RESPONSIBILITY, USEFULNESS and GRACIOUSNESS

from the Caribbean Isle of Jamaica

Copyright © 2014 Edward R. Jo
All rights reserved.

ISBN-10: 9769554103
ISBN-13: 9789769554108

RESPONSIBILITY, USEFULNESS and GRACIOUSNESS

from the Caribbean Isle of Jamaica

a
new spiritual paradigm
for a
new spiritual well-being

Edward R. Johnson

Dedication

This book is dedicated firstly to my deceased parents, Mr. and Mrs. Alfred G. Johnson, who cared and sought for me, all that was considered good for my body and soul. Secondly, my siblings of which I am the fourth of seven and was therefore able to receive from three as I was able to give to three.

Table of Contents

Preface ix
INTRODUCTION xi

Chapter 1. RESPONSIBILITY
1.1 The source of responsibility 1
1.2 Responsibility and construct 8
1.3 Rights construct and deconstruct 9
1.4 Pursuing responsibility 11
1.5 Pursuing of rights 15
1.6 Human development and responsibility 17
1.7 A morality of responsibility 29

Chapter 2. USEFULNESS
2.1 Usefulness and serving 33
2.2 Serving in society through business 43
2.3 Serving in society in state governance 53
2.4 Governance structure 75
2.5 Participatory democratic governance structure 78
2.6 Monitoring of state effectiveness in a participatory democracy 96
2.7 Governance, responsibility and citizenship 100
2.8 The fundamental spirituality of participatory governance 107

Chapter 3. GRACIOUSNESS
3.1 The ground of graciousness 115
3.2 Graciousness and responsibility 116

3.3 Graciousness and religion	120
3.4 Graciousness and civil society	122
3.5 Graciousness and the state	125
3.6 Graciousness and law and order	128
3.7 The moral measure of graciousness	131

Chapter 4. CONTEMPORARY ISSUES

4.1 Issues of morality	137
4.2 Issues of sexual morality	140
4.3 Issues of business morality	146
4.4 Issues of religion and morality	150
4.5 Issue of responsibility through social apprenticeship	153
4.6 Contemporary Caribbean civilization and morality	158
EPILOGUE	161
ABOUT THE AUTHOR	163

Preface

When I was a very young child I collected stamps. My little sister, seeing me do this, started doing so too. As the elder of us two and the one that had started this, it was accepted that I had the privilege; the rights; of first choice of stamps on the letters that came to the family. One day I observed in my sister's collections, what then was a very rare stamp, for which I considered myself as having the rights. While chasing her around the house to take from her these stamps which I considered as being mine, my mother intervened in this child's brawl, took me aside and said that the stamp might well be due to me, but that not because of the material circumstances of our life where it would be difficult to obtain other such stamps that I should be of such poor spirit that I could not allow my little sister to have this one stamp. She taught me then to give, and that material poverty need not be spiritual poverty.

My father was well known to all on the road where we lived for the vigour of his self in the care of his family, one part of which was our schooling. As his children then we had access to the homes of the people there and to the collection of books they had; a library as we considered that then; from which I was loaned books, and which I read enthusiastically.

My family first, and the people along the road on which I lived, made me what I am. I am not perfect, but as we know, there is no perfection in this world of ours. I am reminded of this by my close friends, in particular, who tell me that they see that my parents have tried their best with me, but that I have fallen somehow, and clearly, somewhat short. Today I take responsibility for this as I seek to do what is right and therefore acting responsibly, rather than as I did in earlier times, seeking for my rights. It is in the spirituality of sharing and seeking to enhance the lives of others that we as individuals obtain the true meaning and a positive purpose in one's own life. When we enrich the lives of others, we enrich also our own, as it is in such endeavours that one finds purpose and satisfaction, and from which comes meaning.

It is in this mode of responsibility that I share my thoughts and ideas of that which I am, and from the Caribbean side of the world, with the wider world. One seeks to present to others, these thoughts with the hope that it will assist them in the creating of social structures and systems from which our spiritual values and attitudes are moulded, and which then leads us on to how we live our lives. It is hoped that the thoughts engendered will enable the enrichment of our lives.

In all of this I seek with faith and hope for the intervention of God, the transcendental, imponderable and inexplicable spirit, to make this effort of my sharing, worthwhile for all of us his people.

INTRODUCTION

General

There exists in this world, particularly in those nations in which the western culture is dominant, those who have embraced the philosophy of individualism and its underlying system of thought of the survival of the fittest. The embracing of this philosophy and system of thought, much of it at the subliminal level, and pervasive to our behaviour, has led to a high level of violence, strident sophistry and intellectual dishonesty, an absence of integrity, uncivil behaviour, exercised by ourselves against others, and by ourselves against our self, this latter leading to suicide, whilst the former, leading to the crime of homicide and of wars. Accordingly, it may well be useful for us to stop and think, as is done here, on these matters, as our existence is being diminished through the fear of our fellow human beings in society. By thinking out aloud, and in the presence of others, one seeks to be one's self in keeping with the words of Descartes, "I think therefore I am", By these words he defined his self and his humanity.

In doing this one seeks not only to be, but to share one's humanity with others, as that which we are for the most part, is a function of our society, near and far, and for this we are indebted to our society. Through the act of sharing these thoughts, one hopes to be responsible and to be useful. One hopes too, to be able to accept with graciousness the response to these thoughts, and through all this to be fit to survive.

It is being considered here that we in the western world of what we call post-modern society, and for the engendering of peace in the world at large and the continuity of such, and where each person becomes free from fear of one's fellow human being, accept and embrace the idea of the survival of the fit, rather than of the fittest. In being re-leased from the endeavours to be the fittest and the consequential fears that are engendered in that frame of living with one's fellow human beings, we will then have an increased psychic energy for use in pursuing activities of responsibility, usefulness and graciousness which then give to our lives, purpose, meaningfulness and enrichment.

This thinking out is being done against the background of Jamaica, within the Caribbean part of this diverse universe, and what is considered globalized world. Accordingly, the immediate context of some experiences has been this Jamaican part of the Caribbean, but reflects for a great part a concern of peoples of different nations in this whole world of ours, and our present human condition.

Responsibility

Responsibility, which is discharged through responsible behaviour towards our fellow human beings in society, flows from the fact that our individual humanity that we experience and express is derived from them in our living together. We owe therefore a debt of gratitude to them for whom and what we are, and for that which we experience around us, rather than a forbearance of them, with such priority of privilege for the social space to pursue what we consider to be our rights. This debt lays the ground for each individual to act in a manner that will contribute to the maintaining and enhancement of our human society. This then will be considered individual and human responsibility. It is in the discharging of this human responsibility to our society, beginning from those nearest to us and then farther out to the world and the people there, that we become fit to survive.

Usefulness

Individual responsibility can first be discharged through the use of our ability in deeds that enable the continuity and enhancement of society. Herein lays the idea of usefulness, endeavours which contribute both to the material and spiritual well-being of our fellow human beings in society. In discharging this responsibility of being useful we sit together and decide upon the structure, systems and guidelines within which we will work on a one to one and individual basis, first at the level of the family, next to our near community, and next again at the national and a still further level, the world at large. It is within these rules of engagement we live our lives and which ultimately determines our spirituality, this spirituality being that which obtains at the time these rules of engagement are being determined and also for the most part, by those who determine these rules of, and finally and ultimately too, our law and order

In the activity of creating these rules of engagement, law and order, we find governance of the state. In the activities of serving each other, directly or indirectly; particularly in the satisfying of one's material well-being; we find business. In being useful we give expression to our humanity and its own enhancement, and it goes further to the enhancement of all human beings.

With the acceptance of responsibility and the discharge of this through usefulness in the serving of our fellow human beings in society, near and far, we become fit to survive, and experience personal satisfaction in our life.

Graciousness

Graciousness is an act which allows for the maximizing of the expressions of our humanity and occurs through the enabling contributions of one to another's individual well-being. .The actions of graciousness from others, allows us as individuals more space and support in our pursuit to be responsible and useful. It is within this context that rights flow and also that which is right and what is wrong. The measure of our rights exist therefore in the measure that we behave and act rightfully, and implicit in this is the concept of wrong. One must recognize the occurrence of dysfunctions and aberrations in the universe, and in human behaviour. It is within this frame too that graciousness usually arise, which minimizes the deleterious consequences that come from situations that are aberrant and dysfunctional. Accordingly, acts of graciousness, for the most part enable individuals to be fit to survive, and as best as they can.

It is out of graciousness that civilized behaviour comes. Graciousness, out of which kindliness flows, reinforces in general the acts of responsibility, and by so doing enhances individual well-being and society in general. Graciousness, when sought as rights and privileges either as forbearance or as a duty, demeans and diminish the concept as also our relationships and society. It is further debilitated when pursued without concern for responsibility and with a disconnection from this. In its pursuit in such a manner, civilized society is debased and deconstructed. A house is never built from the top down, but from the bottom upwards.

The ground and the bottom on which we build a civilized society is that of responsibility and usefulness, and its roof is that of graciousness, where we find rights. A house is easily destroyed, when the materials that are used in building is ill-conceived. Rights, which transforms graciousness to duty consequently becomes ill-conceived materials, while acts of graciousness are good materials which create a civilized community; a place where there is a great freedom from fear, and of choice.

Rug

Responsibility, Usefulness and Graciousness make the rug on which we kneel in the presence of God, the transcendental, the inexplicable and imponderable spirit that ultimately moves things in this universe, to give thanks for our lives and our existence within a human and civilized society. It will be one in which, rather than having to be the fittest to survive we are fit to do so through being responsible, useful and gracious.

A civilized society is not obtained in pursuit of our lives in the frame of law and order that is determined by the lower commonality of our humanity, that of our physical and material self, but through our existence within the higher common factor of our humanity, that of our spirituality which flows from our intelligence, and which allows us to be responsible, useful and gracious.

The colours of the rug on which we kneel is black for the strength to bear the burden of responsibility, green for the verdant pastures and places that gives us pleasure in which we find ourselves and in ourselves when we are responsible, and gold for the graciousness of life and living in a civilized community where we are able to express our humanity free from fear, and settle when they occur our conflicts through reason and rational behaviour, rather than through the exercise of physical might.

We begin the process of making our society a civilized one through the nurturing and the educating of young people in their formative years not within a frame and logic of rights, and this in a situation of amorality, but of a morality of responsibility, usefulness and graciousness of one to their fellow human beings in society, and the logic within which we determine what is right and what is wrong.

Chapter I
RESPONSIBILITY

1.1. The source of responsibility

In the latter part of the eighteen century on the continent of Europe a boy was found in the forests living with the wolves there. This boy, later named Victor, the wild boy of Aveyron was captured and considered to be about seven years of age. He had no language then such that he was able to communicate any knowledge or feelings that he had then to the persons who captured him. This was considered capture also, as on seeing his fellow human specie, he ran from then, in order to continue being with the wolves. When he was captured and taken into human society, he ran away repeatedly, and it took some time to have him accepting our human society to be the place for him, and subsequently to learn to read and speak, the latter not particularly well. During the time of his acceptance and adaptation to the human society in which he was then, he was known to have enjoyed being naked and playing out in the snow. It was clear that this young homo-sapiens animal, male human being, and a child, shared not only the physical behaviour of the wolves which was seen in the way he walked and ran, but a commonality of them in respect to their fears and joys such that he preferred being in their society, the wolf pack, rather than that of human society. That was his humanity then.

Aberrant occurrences of human beings falling outside of human society take place as was noted within the recent past when a baby on the African continent was found in the care and protection of a dog. In these aberrations we see clearly and experience God; the transcendental, imponderable and inexplicable spirit; in that of these children not being destroyed by these animals, but being cared for by them, and they returning later to our human society. One's immediate humanity, one's soul and the experience of the transcendental, inexplicable and imponderable spirit of God obtains within a society of human beings. The experience of this spirit of God by the human beings within a society and where they find themselves in this diverse physical world of ours, is the first vector that engenders within each society their religion, that which provides them with the harmony they seek in the pursuit of their material and spiritual existence within the environment in which they find themselves. Human society determines our humanity, what we fear, what we hope and aspire for, and how we experience joy.

In coming to a spiritual being, which we all are; unconsciously or consciously, and unwittingly or wittingly; in a human society, we owe a debt to this society for the humanity that is derived there from. The debt we owe can be seen clearly in the like situation where a person is rescued from drowning by another. In society, the general response and behaviour of a person who has been rescued is for the rescued person to have a feeling of thankfulness and indebtedness to the rescuer, rather than the feeling of the rescuer being indebted to the rescued. In being rescued by God through the expression of his Transcendental, Imponderable and Inexplicable spirit that we find in our universe; and which was expressed through man in this instance; one does not have a right and forbearance against God and man, but gratefulness to them. This is first discharged by being grateful towards one's fellow human being, and then moving on to give expression to this to God. In all of this we see the norm and the fundamental of the behaviour of human being in society as that of recognizing this debt of gratitude which is the ground for the pursuit of responsibility first, rather than the pursuit of rights and privileges firstly.

In the affirming of one's humanity which we acquire from our human society and where we obtain the knowledge that we have and which then determines our beliefs, which then goes further and impacts upon our feelings, we must accordingly accept that we owe to this society into which we are born, generally, a debt of gratitude for this. In this we find patriotism, even to that in which one destroys one's self for the continuity of one's society, and sees this as service to one's society. We owe to our fellow human beings in the street whom we pass each day or once in a lifetime to act in a manner that ensures and enhances that individual's life, and in this way the continuity of our near community, extending then to the far community, and then the world of human beings. It is in our human society, notwithstanding it's imperfections, which impacts upon us that makes us and nurtures us as the individuals that we accept ourselves to be. It is in the pursuit of such actions that affirm our acceptance of responsibility for being part of the process of making our society a better place, a civilized one, for all of us that our rewards and rights occur.

The general pursuit by individuals or groups in society to have the social space to express their humanity within the frame and logic of the fact that they are human beings, the physical and lower common vector of our human self; not that of the higher vector of intelligence from which a spirituality is derived and which enables one to adjust to the environment in which they find themselves, of this diverse universe of ours; and considering this the grounds for their rights, is in essence the seeking of rewards without endeavours. In the situation where rewards and benefits are not generally espoused for responsible behaviour, but more so in the matter of forbearance, and deferential treatment within the frame of rights, this becomes dysfunctional and deleterious, not only to the society in general in the form of our relationships to each other there, but paradoxically so, to our own self. Firstly, such a person will be perceived as one who wishes to receive without giving and acting therefore in the diminishing of the well-being of society, and considered therefore of low spirituality and character. As the numbers of these increase, material well-being decreases and survival rests upon the annihilating of others, and where the survival of the fittest becomes the mantra and basis for our existence. Secondly, in this we then create for ourselves a human jungle and demean our lives.

In the proclamation and acclamation of individual rights as that coming first in the enabling of ourselves to live as individuals or in special sub-groups, or groups, and that this is fundamental to our humanity and existence, we unwittingly and inexorably move to the deconstruct of a civilized society. When we create in society the law and consequential order which determines how organizations there must function all of these institutions then determining how we live our life in society, and with this spirituality of rights being first rather than responsibility, there will be embedded in society amongst the people there a spirituality where receiving is more important for their existence than that of contributing and serving. In due course the institutions fall apart and later the society. The spirituality or rights and rewards from society without responsibility demean and diminish individuals and our humanity, and removes purpose and meaning in one's existence. It is the situation in which annihilation thrives, and the engendering of a spirituality that could be considered nihilism. It is within this logic and spirituality too, that the winner takes all exist, and which is a feature of the structuring of much of our western government institutions.

In the pursuit of responsibility first, we move to the construct of society, and quite quickly so. In the spirituality of responsibility where we use our talents and creativity in the serving of others in society, be it in private or public business enterprises, or in the governance of the state and which from out of these endeavours, we obtain our equitable rewards, as we also obtain purpose, meaning and satisfaction in our lives.

In the activities of serving others through whatever role we do this, either within a business enterprise, a state organization, or in the governance of the state, and in the context of our co-existence to our human family, beginning with our biological one, then to the clan, then to the tribe, or the ethnic group, next to the nation, and finally to the world, the need arises for rules and regulations that will guide our relationships. The rules and regulations which are espoused by the state are considered our law and order and the essence of governance and they ultimately determine the spirituality and humanity of generally all, within the state. In a business organization, this spirituality is generally considered its culture. Today's state governance has evolved from within the framework of thinking of the survival of the fittest and from earlier times where we existed some of us as serfs, bondsmen, or slaves, others as free men, warriors warlords, tribal chiefs lords dukes and kings, and in our later days here within the sphere and control of community dons, all controlling and determining the social reality and relationships of our community and which impact on our lives more so than that of the law and order of our state and nation. We now have there what is known as representative democracy, and particularly so in western societies, where we no longer exist as slaves, but as the commodity of human capital.

In the representative democracies in which we now live our lives, and as was espoused by Plato for his city states and where the representatives were selected by the guardian class there, and not the others living in these states, representative democracy then was also a participatory one. The representatives then were near and deeply connected to each other in those small city states societies. It was for this reason that persons as representatives, giving service to the state in its governance had to remove themselves from their families in order that they serve the people and the state in the most objective manner; for the benefit of the many, rather than a selected or near few. Along the way and as societies grew and representatives represented larger groups: constituent; the participatory dimension of what was sought in a democratic government for its citizens, became less so. One did not see one's representative near enough or often enough to be able to talk with, or to interact with and to become aware of the daily life of the community and their perspectives for which they had the responsibility to represent in the developing of the law and order within which they would have to live their life. This disconnection was the first dilemma in representative democracy, which arose out of the well-being and growth of communities and society.

Another dilemma was the formation of sub-groups with special interests, and where these persons of special interests did not all reside in one community. To represent these groups and interests, and in a situation of disconnection of the representative from their community, and seeking to hold them all together as one, it became necessary for those who sought to be a representative of the people in the governance of the state, to be all things to all of these groups through some common factor, often times in a situation of contradiction and of conflict.. It became too, for those who sought to be and who became a representative of a constituency, usually then of people of varying and conflicting interests, for this representative to be more of their own self and psychological integrity, whatever that integrity was. The selection of a representative therefore, became the expression of the people in so far that the integrity of the person was more accepted by the people of a constituency. In many cases this integrity has become more that of a manipulative one for survival in the selective process, spiritually or materially, and as congruent with the pervasive value system and thinking of a society of the survival of the fittest. It is in this manipulative mode towards the broadest seam of interest, that the most common factor of our existence, that we are all human beings, on which our rights have been constructed. The construct does not bring with it our intelligence from which our spirituality obtains and allows us to be responsible members of society. In this division of our physical and mental self, we place ourselves in the situation where our material and physical self becomes the major factor in our existence and where the survival of the fittest is enabled by this physical self. Paradoxically, when rights were given to all, it was in fact seeking to establish that all were fit to survive, but this was without the concern of our intelligence which is a major dimension of our humanity and which has allowed us to evolve as we have done. It is when we use our intelligence not to destroy but to enhance the condition of all, acting responsibly that we best adjust to our environment. Our human condition is enhanced in this situation and as it enables all to be fit to survive.

In the pursuit of existence without any responsibility for anything but one's own well-being; whatever this may be; within the frame given of forbearance and rights, our human existence has been placed in the frame of the survival of the fittest. All this has led towards the deconstruction of society as a civilized place and the creating of a human jungle. When we pursue responsibility firstly in the things that we do, it is then that we enhance our human condition and create civilized communities and societies

1.2. Responsibility and construct.

The acceptance that one's humanity is derived from our existence in a human society, allows us to give thanks to the divine spirit of God, the Transcendental, Inexplicable and Imponderable, for life and living, where we are and how we are. We worship him therefore according to how he expresses Himself to us in the society where we find ourselves and where we are situate in this universe. We then ask, given who and what we are, and with what we have, how does one fulfill one's debt of gratitude for our existence and contribute to the maintaining and enhancing of the society and the human beings therein.

In recognizing the material and the spiritual aspects of nature, we seek opportunities therein to contribute and by so doing discharge our debt and responsibility to God through service to our fellow human beings and society. Immediately that we do this; and use our talents such as we have, and whatever they may be; we begin the process of construct and development. In seeking to construct, build and develop we may recognize frailties in our self as an individual and that in order to overcome such it is a good thing to work with others and group of likeminded persons to make our contributions. This cohesion of persons help further in constructive actions and allows too for the diminishing of differences between these persons, and this is particularly so when they share the experience of achieving goals that they as an individual could not have achieved. In this we find social cohesion, and a spirituality that reduces the differences that may exist between each other. The bonds between these persons are further deepened when these activities enhance goals that are important to the wider human society. The act of accepting at the individual level a responsibility for contributing to society, and which when it leads to creating capacity in one's self for working with others thereby giving rise to the concept and expression of collective responsibility; communal living; firstly creates in the individual a spiritual well-being as it also enhances their civility. As meaning and purpose comes into the life of individuals we find here people who are fit to survive, and who will then create a society that provides each person with not only a spiritual well-being, but also that of a satisfying material well-being. It is in this mode that we construct a civilized and civil society, that of the pursuit of responsibility.

I.3. Rights construct and deconstruct

When we ask for rights, be it individual or human, we ask for forbearance and entitlements from and of others for us to be whom and what we are, and having the social space in which to satisfy one's wishes for one's existence. This begins and ends in one's self. Whether we ask this of God or of our fellow human beings in society, we implicitly seek to establish ourselves, either individually or as a group, as being not as others, more so or less so. In the insistence of this entitlement and forbearance, regardless of how it discommodes and diminishes the life space of others, we set the ground for the deconstruction of society as a civilized place, within the logic of the survival of the fittest. The fittest then will be those who are best able to diminish and demean others to obtain and sustain the life for which they consider they have a right to. The tools for this will be guns and other such weapons together with sophistry and intellectual dishonesty. It is in this context that persons, politicians, in the quest for the opportunity to serve a constituent of persons as their representative in their governance process, proffer patronage to them through empathizing with these desires, and as is wished by the individuals or groups within this constituent, to have these satisfied, usually by the granting of rights. These persons in the pursuit of serving the nation do not proffer themselves to a constituent of people as a point of focus for the facilitating of a group of persons to serve each other, and to be creative, responsible and useful in endeavours that will not only enhance the lives of the people of these individual constituents, but also the society in general and of which they are a part. In the pursuit of these rights and entitlements; many of which are considered to be human rights; given to them through patronage, and usually in a unidimensional framework without concern for responsibility, no regard is given for the reality of the mental dimension of our human selves and as the major determining vector in the engendering of our humanity now or in the future, forcing forbearance and precedence of one's self over others in perpetuity. When these individuals fail to obtain the rights of their choice they consider themselves victims of society, the place wherein they obtained their humanity, and their fellow human beings, oppressors.

When we pursue rights, whether they are considered divine or human, we are in fact asking for a share of that which is available then, and which was made possible through the endeavours of others before us, and an entitlement to such. When this is done in a unidimensional manner without concern for responsibility, we diminish our material well-being and demean our humanity and spiritual well-being. There may well be some construct for some while, but within a short time, deconstruct of social space for all begins. As we take without contributing or concern for this, might becomes the tool for the measuring of equity within the system of thought of the survival of the fittest. This demeans us materially and spiritually.

The latency for the deconstruction of a civilized society exists within this system of thought and consequential actions. When it matures and becomes overt, its expression is then seen in the pervasive violence around us which leads us to a general fear of our fellow human beings in society. We move to the deconstruction of civilized society when we pursue rights first and above all things and too, in a unidimensional manner

1.4. Pursuing responsibility.

In the pursuit of responsibility and the consequential search to contribute to society one places one's self on the path to becoming useful and this then gives purpose and meaning to one's life. In this mode we seek to develop relationships and structures that will enable us to reach this goal, and all these actions construct and enhance our human situation. We have relationships first between individuals within the family, and in this we at all times seek to be responsible by being fair and equitable, honest and trusting of each other as we contribute to the well-being of each other there. This then becomes the pattern of our behaviour and character, our humanity and within this mode we then seek to contribute to our community. In the pursuit of responsibility we place ourselves on the path to the creating and the construct of bonds between people and the fostering of a humanity that enables a community and society later, of civilized people.

As is nature and of the Spirit of God, there occurs in most things, and this includes too our human interactions and relationships, from time to time, aberrations and dysfunctions. This is part of our ultimate not-knowingness, and a commonality of our humanity and human existence. For this reason we need structures and an approach not only to deal with these occurrences that from time to time diminish the positive measure of our responsible actions, but also to assist in ensuring the continuity of our responsibility and contributions to society.

Within the occurrences in nature of that which is conceptualized as negative and positive, Sir Francis Bacon in his unfinished writings in "Novum Organum" has construed positive vectors of thought from occurrences that are conceptualized as negative, and which enables people in society to have power over nature. In this we see clearly, the duality of nature, that of good coming from bad, and as it too clearly establishes the concept of that negative and positive, good and bad. In the minimalist construct of good and bad we then have perspectives of right and wrong; that which enhances and that which diminishes. In this simple and dual construct we have saint and sinners, honourable and dishonourable, material and spiritual, individualism and collectivism, left and right, black and white. It is an accepted postulate such that any person that one should meet on the street in society would agree with the idea that it is easier to walk on a straight path on the colours of black which denotes the burdens life and which engenders strength, or on that of white, which denotes purity and the fragility of life which engenders sensitivity, as one's footstep can be easily seen there to guide in the path considered straight.. It is however considered much more difficult to walk in a straight path on the colour of grey, which is the blending of black and white, as one will not see so clearly their footsteps that can guide their walking. It is accepted by most people in society, that it is more so in the shades of grey in which the truth lie, rather than in black that is usually considered wrong or white, usually considered right. To make the best of our human situation and dilemma, if we must err, and as is nature there is no perfection and errors; aberrations; occur as we pursue our goals in life, it is better to do so in pursuit of doing what is considered right, rather than to do so in pursuit doing what is considered wrong.

Given the existence of the minimalist construct of duality of one sort or another in all the things that we do, and that of right or wrong in the managing the affairs of our life, we need structures that enable us to exist within this situation and norm of nature, that will reduce as best as possible the errors and dysfunctions that will arise. We need structures in our families, in our near and far communities and extending to our nation that enables the perspectives that exist within these groups to be heard and to be used in the determining of the path and road we travel in the pursuit of our existence. Such structures should enable us to hear with continuity the diverse voices and perspectives of those who must exist within a given social space, out of which we will then take decisions which we modify as we evolve and recognize potential and occurring flaws that arises from time to time. In the pursuit of the goal of us living together it will be seen that it is when we individually consider our existence not as that which is different from others, and for which a social space must be given for the pursuit of our special and diverse well-being and wishes, but as one whom seeks to make a contribution to our human condition, that this enhances our human situation. It is the situation in which we all are able to survive, not having to be the fittest to do so, but rather being fit to do so. As we pursue our lives within the frame of the enhancing our collective human situation and society, we accordingly display a sense of responsibility for our general human condition and as we become too, useful members of society. It then is being a responsible person that enables one fit to survive, rather than having to be the fittest.

In the pursuit of being responsible, we as individuals look at the needs of our fellow human beings and seek to satisfy such as we are able to do. We exist in families, extended ones that reaches out to become our nation and we seek to serve, recognizing and accepting that our individual self is ultimately served by our family of human beings, and that being useful in serving is our contribution to one's human condition and situation. We will find that our individual human condition and situation is best served, not by diminishing the social space and humanity of others, but by the enhancing of these dimensions of our human existence, and as too, it also provides more scope for each to do so.

While being responsible and consequentially useful in society, we will recognize differences in our individual selves; the nature of our diversity; talents, competencies, character all determining our humanity, that which we will seek to use for making our collective contribution to the enhancement of our collective human situation. In this process, because we seek to build, our fellow human beings and society provides us with rights, entitlements, and forbearance in accord with our contributions. We create through this a society within the concept of the survival of the fit and would have moved away from the purely material and physical value that determines our human survival as that of being the fittest and which is the lower dimension of our humanity. We then move to the higher dimension where our spirituality exists and which has enabled the adjustments of our diverse selves to our environment, and has enabled our survival, fit to survive; in this diverse world of ours. It is the spiritual dimension of our humanity which enables us systems of thoughts and morality that enables the creating of civilized societies.

I.5. Pursuing of rights.

In the pursuing of rights this is done constructively within the frame and logic of responsibility where in collaborating with others and recognizing too our individual talent; and the consequential differences and capacity in contributing to the general well being of our human society; we seek to ascertain that no person is diminished through not being given the opportunity to be useful. It is within this frame of thought of the survival of the fit, that we obtain and pursue rights and entitlement. In accepting from each person that which they contribute, we behave graciously as we also increase the sum total of the possibilities for the enhancement of our society. We have here self interest, not one that is centered around one self's, even to it being the determination of self worth, but an interest that enables one to be part of the enhancement of the human condition of the community, and from which forbearance and rights are sought. We serve and are served by being provided rights, entitlement and forbearance. When through actions of responsibility for our human situation, we work to enhance this, and we do so with others, advantaged or disadvantaged, we go further along the path of service to self and the society, and become, even more fit to survive. The pursuits of rights, becomes then an instrument for the enabling of usefulness not only of one's self but of others and it enhances society and makes it a more civilized one.

The pursuit of rights in this manner creates and provide the social space where there is engendered in individuals, greater usefulness and contributions of the people in general, whilst not diminishing others and as it constructs a civilized society where the material and spiritual well being of all people there are considered and becomes better for all.

The pursuit of rights which ends in the individual and with a disconnection from responsibility creates a situation of conflict and chaos which later provides the ground where survival is of the might of the fittest. In this frame of the might of the fittest violence, sophistry the demeaning and diminishing of others and the exalting of one's self occurs. In this disconnect between rights and responsibility; the physical and material dimension on one side of our humanity and the mental and spiritual dimension on the other side of it; and might even to that used in communication; we coarsen our lives as we deconstruct our society as a civilized place, and make it into a human jungle. When our material and physical self is considered more important than our mental and spiritual self, this latter is then used in the frame in which it is most rewarding, not for the enhancing of society, but in the determining and the identifying of our self, either as one within a likeminded group, and or individual. In a human jungle society where might is right, either wittingly or unwittingly and this through default; choice and charity will be removed from it and kindliness becomes a duty for some, usually those who do not have what then is might, the mighty. We reduce our freedom to act kindly or charitably, when such acts are transformed into a duty of forbearance to others and as rights, and create in people there a sense of alienation, not only of one for the others, but for those who are identifiable the mighty, and who determines the spirituality of their social space. This creates a situation of chaos, and one which takes a direction towards existing generally outside of the accepted norms and parameters of the society, and even of that which is considered the norms of nature, as then it is the might required of the moment that determines one's behaviour and actions for survival, and as the fittest.

In a situation of the pursuit of rights in a purist manner all our relationships becomes exploitative ones, where sophistry and might becomes the tools for survival. It is congruent with the system of thought of the survival of the fittest. In this disconnect from responsibility which is the mental and spiritual dimension of our humanity, which enables and facilitates our adjustment to the environment in which we find ourselves, this leads to the construct of human jungle society, and the deconstruction of one in which we find a civilized citizenry. It is when we pursue our human rights with a mental and consequential spiritual connect that brings it into the frame of responsibility, that we construct and create the civilized the society that we wish.

I.6. Human development and responsibility

The process of an individual's development begins within one's self and through an acceptance of responsibility for one's own self, the recognition of one's position in life, one's talent, and giving thanks for one's humanity. In Jamaica, we do not in sufficient numbers now accept responsibility for ourselves and one's position in life. An expression of this is evidenced by stating that the situation of the society is that of the making of the governments, they being responsible for all the ills that befalls us, and the correction of these with requital too, all resting with the government. No one in society is responsible for, or contributes to the wrong doing that obtains; not even for the selection of the government whom as a nation we have chosen to govern us. This is particularly so when it is considered that this is being done badly. It will be said by a constituent when it becomes clear that the representative, whom they have selected to represent them in the process of their governance, may be or is flawed, that they were manipulated. When flawed behaviour is seen in a number of the representatives and too in the governance of the nation, the people of nation will then say that they were all manipulated. Accepting that manipulative actions do occur, one asks the question, why is it necessary to have persons who wish to serve them having to manipulate them to be selected to do so, and are there not parameters outside of which they can be manipulated. This brings the answer, that the representative reasonably represents and reflects in general the character of the people; constituents first and nation next. When therefore we accept responsibility for the choice we make in the persons we seek to represent us and consequently the quality of governance that we have, we go further in the process of our development and of our humanity and self.

Another step that we can take in this process, and perhaps the greatest one, is that of acknowledging the responsibility of some of our kith and kin for us being here, arriving here as slaves for most of us, and being exploited. We know of the grief and agony of our journey here through the Middle passage. We should however ask ourselves how did we get on to those ships and in the manner that we did and to be transported here; might there not have been collaboration and complicity of our brothers in the situation; naively or not so naively, wittingly or unwittingly; for whatever benefits that may have accrued to them and accordingly accomplices and beneficiaries then in the matter. The ships that took us from amongst our kith and kin, left from the docks and we all did not live in and around these docks, so we had to be found and taken from the interior and country side, there. There are those who no doubt visited the ships at the docks and knew the manner in which we would be traveling. We can be mindful too that though slavery was abolished from this side, more so than from elsewhere and also within the world as globalized then, where prevailing conditions and situations of interest and of conflicts impacted on the matter of slavery, there were brothers and sisters of ours who had come here on the ships as others did and who shared in the experience and agony of the travel, who gave assistance to the maintaining of the condition of enslavement for others. We have been actively participating in the creating of our human condition and spirituality. This acknowledgement enables us to remove from ourselves negative feeling and emotions that we have, some contrived, and for us to be more rational in dealing with our present and real situation. It allows us to accept responsibility for our lives, as it engenders in us an integrity and humanity of strength that enhances and make us more civilized as a people and nation.

Slavery has been a part of our human history. There were slaves in the Greek City States, for whom it was not espoused that they should vote in the selection of the representatives in Plato's considered democratic state, and from where we obtained our first concept of democracy. We know too of the Greek city Sparta, a most austere and militaristic one, which controlled a part of Greece, where the people kept their selves in a fit and athletic condition, part of which was to control their slaves. Nevertheless, this state was overthrown by Thebes, another Greek city state, where the leader had then recently released the slaves under their control. We know of Englishmen who were taken slaves on the

Barbary Coast during the same time that Africans were being transported to the new land here. When we accept the fact of the history of human beings exploiting others in various forms, slavery as in Greece and the West Indies; serfdom as in Russia, bondsmen in England, and that we were not innocent bystanders in our own case and the creating of this earlier situation in the Caribbean, West Indies, and the resolution of this to the evolution of ourselves to where we are now existing in independent states and nation, we can recognize and accept that we have progressed. We can note too that there has been progress in Greece, Russia and England and some commonality in our humanity. Within the context of the fact that we have progressed, and the commonality of the expression of our humanity in this world, we can accept responsibility for our condition and ask ourselves what further we can do for ourselves to further help and improve our human situation.

When we look at our talents and resources within our environment and we ask ourselves how do we use these talents and resources and the environment to enhance ourselves, we will find then that the answer lies in our becoming useful in giving service to others, firstly in and amongst ourselves, and then to our outer world at large through such industry that we are able to create. We then go further and ask ourselves as individuals how do we individually, make ourselves able to serve. In accepting responsibility we begin on the road to our empowerment; that which we do for ourselves to improve our condition, and which is the true meaning of empowerment. In accepting responsibility for one's self and condition, an individual places one's self on the path to their development as that is the tool which empowers one to deal with the changes required for one's self to enable the pursuit of actions that will enable the enhancement and development of one's human condition then.

Rights and consequential forbearance that is given to one and as is parallel to patronage, does not give empowerment as this comes not from others but from within ourselves as we accept responsibility for our own selves. Rights and forbearance flows from patronage, and as is expressed in the notion of tolerance, as it entraps and further enslaves the patronized one who then is diminished, rather than empowered. The pursuit of responsibility empowers and develops where the pursuit of rights enslaves and diminishes. The underlying spiritual force and attribute of progress, moving on and upwards, is the positive thinking that is engendered when one accepts one's responsibility for one's self and situation. This thinking, wittingly or unwittingly allows for the reconciliation of differences, an example of which was done and seen in our Southern African nation family. This enabled people to work together to resolve problems that were found in their immediate life and living and which had to be overcome to make it better for all, now and later.

One feels that Sam Sharpe and Paul Bogle, heroes of Jamaica, thought positively and wittingly so and took responsibility into their own hands then to resolve their situation and for us other today who are their forbears. We go further in the resolution of our human problems and the enhancement of our situation when we take responsibility for ourselves and conditions, rather than to exploit the past agony and situation of our forbears. It is not now slavery which Sam Sharpe put an end to, nor an European upper class which Paul Bogle put an end to, nor our colonial masters from which we gained Independence, nor a past or prevailing government fault that we ourselves selected to govern us, nor the globalized world in which we are but a little village that determines our condition. These situations however, provide us with a ground of negatives and positives, out of which we determine for ourselves, our condition and direction. When we become encumbered by the negatives and engage totally the mental and psychic energies that is a part of our fundamental humanity, in the creation of rights, forbearance and indulgence which is not the frame in which a good character is built, but deal with the positives that has arisen therein and this by the acceptance of responsibility for our present situation, this engenders in us the energies to solve the problems that now exists in our present environment and impacts upon us, now and for the future. Actions flowing from the acceptance of responsibility for ourselves and the payment of the debt of gratitude to our forbears for who and what we are enables us to spiral upwards in our humanity, and in this we create and construct an environment where we can as civilized persons develop and become even more so. It is one in which we seek to be useful members of society and which will enable future citizens to seek to repay us in like manner that we repay our forbears. In all of this we find that as we develop our individual humanity by being responsible and consequently useful, we obtain development in our society as it spirals upward, enhancing our human condition, and become a civilized community, one wherein we live in peace for most of us with each and fear few if any.

We of Jamaica, land of wood and water, have inherited a place in this universe that is bountiful and beautiful, even more so than that which one finds in Africa where there is to be found savannahs and boundless animals. There is an awesomeness that is experienced in the vastness and aridity of the desert savannahs, as there is the beauty of our land, both of which are the work of God.

Our land is peopled mainly by human beings who are a blending of persons from every continent of the world, the black race and the white race, the yellow and the brown; and in religions, the Jews, the Christians, the Muslims, the Hindus, to name a few, all these making us firstly Jamaican, and of some very near similarity of our fellow Caribbean people, and next, a very talented people. This character of being talented occurs, as anthropology, the study of mankind tells us, when diverse group of people merge, they become so, and stronger. It is this very group of merged people that later becomes known as a pure people, such as the Nazis of Germany considered themselves to be. This concept of a pure people is fallacious, and given the fact that strength obtains in diversity, it can be accepted that the pursuit of such purity is destructive, as is evidenced by the deleterious situation of incest, which can be considered an extended point in the pursuit of the purity of a human group of people.

Slavery for the Caribbean peoples carry with it a strong negative emotional tenor that seeks the avoidance of its recurrence in the pursuit of forbearance against all, and this is reflected in the eminence of rights in all societal systems and structures. It allows for the creating of scapegoats, and also at times, hallucinatory endeavours. To the extent that individuals pursue any of these activities in their life and living, to that extent they diminish in general their survival capacity. When groups or communities do so, they diminish their community and society and their own individual humanity. It is in this diminished situation where in the pursuit of such activities that provides us with life and living that one seeks within the frame of rights and forbearance, entitlement and patronage all for the making of one's life a better one, and in the achievement of the goals the individual seeks. When this is provided in the context of the utilitarian principle of the greatest good for the greatest number, with each person or group determining that which is good for them selves without concern for others, we move further and more quickly to societal deconstruct as the social space for each is demeaned and by so doing, diminished.

In the pursuit of the governance of the state where rights are more important than responsibility one finds a heightened likelihood for conflicts and possible contradictions. In giving patronage to persons who are dysfunctional in their behaviour, such as those who steal or use drugs for the purpose of hallucinating, in the pre-eminence of what is considered their human rights, catering only to the physical dimension of their humanity and not of the mental and consequential spirituality of our humanity where we find responsibility, a disconnect occurs. This has deleterious consequences as it diminishes the value of the spiritual dimension of our humanity and the consequential character of responsibility. One moves in the direction of the deconstruction rather than the construct of a civilized society. The fact of being a human animal is not that of itself which engenders the continuity and development of human society, but that of being of a spirituality and character of responsibility from which this can obtain.

The continuity of our human existence, and together, rests upon the responsibility that is shared by each for others, rather than for one to be the fittest and above others. Development of one's humanity flows from our existence together, and further development rests upon the cumulative individual growth. Individual growth does not occur when patronage is given in the lowering of standards, and particularly so in respect of our education, which hones the use of our human mental capacity, and from which the spiritual dimension of our humanity is derived. In a number of societies now considered modern and progressive, this has been so. In these societies in search for providing rights for all in education, and also self worth of young persons who pass through the structures, concern is given more to the physical dimension of their humanity in the determining of standards and privilege, rather than the development of their mental talent; with paradoxically so, the predisposition towards the abstract of such more valued, than that of the predisposition towards the concrete, the physical and material self and from which one's rights flows. The consequence, is that in these societies, an increasing percentage of these young persons have been unable to contribute their society and are found to be in a situation of impoverishment both material and spiritual which reflects in their behaviour of alienation, and as is reflected in their use of hallucinatory drugs. This is seen in the increased and general use of the drugs legally, for what is deemed generally, as medicinal purposes. Behaviour that occurs during the time of hallucination places one's self at risk and others too, and when concern is given more to the protecting of what is the rights of a hallucinating person in the frame of what is considered their human rights, more than that which is given to the person not hallucinating and the protecting of such persons, unwittingly we give more value to hallucinatory behaviour and those who do so, than others not hallucinating and who do not do so. When hallucinatory behaviour is recognized and action is taken to assist one in correcting this, through the enhancement of the situation of the individual which created the ground for their alienation and consequential behaviour of alienation, this is more beneficial to the individual and to society. Society would have accepted responsibility for the individual's behaviour and in this sought a correction that redounded to the individual first and then to the society. In this manner the individual and society is enhanced.

When in seeking to hone our mental skills by the educating of citizens and when they are near to the adult stage, more consideration is placed in going through the process rather than the outcomes of this in their reasoning competence on one hand and learning on the other, this to enable these young persons to have a sense of achievement; self worth; the process of reducing the capacity of society to satisfy its material and spirituality is commenced. It also impacts negatively on the spirituality of the individual, and then collectively, the society. It is in our mental well being where our spirituality exists and our ultimate humanity which allows us to evolve, through adapting and adjusting to the diverse environments in which we find ourselves and in which we seek a harmony of life and living. When the physical and human dimension of our self is prioritized above our mental and spiritual one, might is made the source and essence of right. This brings us to the mantra of the survival of the fittest and responsibility of little or no value, this latter being that which is the ground in which collaborative endeavours is engendered and which then creates a civilized society.

In the Jamaican society the political elite came to power and replaced the colonial elite of the near slave society, through what then was the championing of the rights of the people in society. In this manner power as was sought, provided to this new elite the capacity to select from the people those with whom they would wish to work with in service to the people and nation within state institutions. They selected then persons that were well known to them, and whom they could trust to act as was considered fitting and at times, according to the guidance they would give them when serving in these institutions. In this manner power was transferred to the new elite, all this then being considered as development.

In the providing of rights for each against the other without any concern for responsibility, and next the giving of opportunities to others to serve because of one being likeminded of the other and to whom guidance can be best given, than that of opportunities to those who have subject competence and skills, substance such as perhaps may have existed before, has been replaced with form and in this we find not only the power of patronage, but also cronyism and corruption.

The reality is that over time though there has been some improvement in our material well being, the general quality of life for people has been diminished, and particularly so in what obtains in the wider western societies of which we consider ourselves to be a part. This is evidenced firstly, by the level of our material well being, even with the improvements that have occurred in this; the lowering of motivation and interest amongst citizens to use their talent or creativity towards being useful, and also the generally lower numbers of persons that can be considered educated. This in a circular manner reduces these individuals capacity to be useful and from which they can obtain meaning and purpose in their lives and subsequent self worth. In respect of society, this lends itself to the occurrence of a level of crime and violence there which engenders fear for our fellow citizens. When within such a society it is considered that survival rests upon being the fittest and the fittest is more physical than spiritual and this is entrenched in the law and order of the society in the frame of human rights, it moves towards becoming a human jungle, rather than a civilized one. Human development flows more so from one's individual self within a group of human beings rather than from one's self outside of a group and accordingly marginalized, and to the extent that one contributes to the enhancement of this group, rather than seeking entitlement and forbearance from others, to that extent is the individual able to develop their individual self and capabilities. Behaviour and character developed within the frame of rights diminishes more than it enhances, whilst within that of responsibility and usefulness enhances more than it diminishes.

Development of one's self, and cumulatively society, generally flows from responsibility and responsible behaviour from each individual there, and such behaviour comes first from one's mental and spiritual self. This is enhanced when combined with the knowledge that exists there and with the combination of this with one's talent in the pursuit of being useful. In giving concern first to responsibility, we ask this of ourselves and are able to begin immediately on the tasks that enable development and we then we go on to assist others to do so. Within the paradigm of responsibility, and the pursuit of such, we enhance our lives and society and our individual human competence and capacity. When we pursue this we find the greatest of personal satisfaction and accordingly the enhancement of our humanity and development at the individual level, which is the basis for the development of society in general. When we go further to help others to accept the pursuit of responsibility in their lives, we deepen the satisfaction in our lives and living as too we enhance the quality of life in society.

It is the acceptance of responsibility for one's self that makes a positive difference in our life, and which makes one seeks to be useful, rather than to seek one's rights. Psychic energies used in the establishing of rights limits and debilitates, whereas such energy used in the discharge of responsibility creates, enhances and develop our human and individual condition and consequentially, society; now for our selves and later for our forbears. We become a civilized nation then which facilitates our material development. It is seen therefore that society develops primarily through the pursuit of individual responsibility, and out of which flows what then can be considered to be human rights, and better considered as civil rights. Such rights enables civil conduct of our relationships in society, and which is above and beyond that which flows from the physical and material dimension of our humanity on which human rights exist, and this with a disconnect from our spiritual self. Society is best developed within the frame of responsibility, leading to civil rights and the frame within which our mental and spiritual self and our material and spiritual self can be balanced, rather than in the unidimensional pursuit of our physical being within the frame of human rights.

I.7. A morality of responsibility.

For the most part and for most of us, the first vector of a system of thought and morality that determines the correctness and appropriateness of our responses in our relationship with our fellow human beings in society is that of our individual rights that allows us entitlement and forbearance. This prioritizes our physical and material self, and it extends and promotes material well- being where the display of the materials that we possess becomes a dimension of this, rather than our mental and spiritual self from which comes our greater capacity to adapt and evolve. The provision of human rights to all could be considered a societal act of graciousness to correct and reduce the dysfunctional aspects of the pursuit of life within the frame of thought of the survival of the fittest. The second vector arises out of our ultimate not-knowingness, this being extrapolated within a sophist frame of argumentation, that immediate outcomes that are dysfunctional and deleterious cannot be used to determine if an act is right or wrong, as given the duality of nature, we ultimately cannot conceive the end results of our actions and of things. We pursue our existence within these vectors, the first of which is the survival of the fittest and the other of graciousness that gives rights to all of us, this within a situation of not-knowingness. These rights becomes enforceable through the law and order then where might, physical and mental; and in which there is no morality of what is right or what is wrong, determines the regulations of this law and order. In a circular manner, such law and order engenders a constant struggle and consequential chaos within society, where there is the continuing fight for survival through being the fittest.

It is in the struggle of being the fittest now that violence occurs, and which is engendered in our sophist argumentation of not being able to recognize what is right and what is wrong and a basis for the development of moral standards for the determining of human character and behaviour. By default then right becomes the tolerance of all that obtains, and the morality, which, when this is pursued with strident might that then is the norm of life and living, society is demeaned as it places itself on the road to becoming a human jungle, where the quality of life for all there is materially and spiritually coarsened. We diminish rather than enhance our lives, in all of this.

A human being is born an infant in society. And for the most part, without fear, and life is considered rich when one experiences little or no fear of one's fellow human beings as one goes about one's daily life, using one's talents in being useful and in the expression of one's humanity. The Caribbean citizens experiences the absence of fear or very little for their neighbours at a very deep level due to the overcoming of slavery in their near past and the fact of them sharing their near social space, a diversity of people from all continents of the world within their small island states. In the general absence of racial or ethnic fear of one's fellow human beings, individuals express to all people a generosity and warmth in life and living. A morality derived from the commonality of behaviour where there is the absence of fear of one's fellow human beings and fellow citizens, and where there is the acceptance of the diversity of our nature and human beings, accordingly easily engenders graciousness and is rewarding and enhances life. The graciousness that exists is not engendered out of the pursuit of rights and the forbearance of one person against the other, but is engendered out of the commonality of concern and care for each other and from which the continuity of their existence arises, that being the expression of responsibility, and for each other. Out of this, flow the spirituality and a morality which creates law and order there that deepens the absence of fear and enriches our lives.

In all of this we recognize the ultimate not-knowingness of the far end consequences of the things we do, even as we perceive the immediate functionality of outcomes which we desire and which we identify as good and right. Other outcomes which we do not wish and are in general dysfunctional as they deconstruct and diminish our situation of life, we identify as bad and wrong. From this we consequently create our morality of right and wrong and later the ground on which law and order in society is determined. Law and order in society would then ultimately rest, not on the generally balanced immediate outcomes of deconstruct or tendencies for this in the pursuit of rights, and this particularly so when it is done unidimensionally, but on the generally balanced immediate outcomes of construct or tendencies for this in the pursuit of responsibility. The societal correct of graciousness would exist within this context, as it enhances the lives of the people in the pursuit of responsibility for one another, and the enrichment and continuity of our humanity and human society where as a civilized place we experience little or no fear of our fellow citizens.

Chapter 2
USEFULNESS

2.1. Usefulness and serving
The spirituality of usefulness

Young persons nearing the time when they will be required to accept fully the responsibility for their individual material well- being and thinking within the frame of the acceptable norms and values of society, think in diverse ways. A significant number give thought to this in a generalized form by accepting and doing whatever job they obtain with the only criteria for undertaking this being the monetary rewards that satisfies their material needs and aspirations. There are however amongst these young adults those who give thought to their survival and pursuit of this in the context of a career within a considered profession, usually a job of social merit and significance and which have established certain knowledge boundaries that guides one in its undertaking. The reward of such jobs is usually both materially and spiritually satisfying, the latter aspect being more in the esteem in which the job is regarded in society. In a career of politics or religion the paramount concern is usually the spirituality of service rather than the materialism of the monetary rewards there from. In the pursuit of a career in politics, success and rewards in this is highly dependent on others, whilst in the career of religion, this is more dependent on one's self than on others.

Outside of these two eminent careers of spiritual service for which the needs are generally few in society, and accordingly limited to a few persons, the general approach towards our existence is within the spiritual paradigm of thought of the survival of the fittest where the situation has become depersonalized as one seeks to become the best human capital available to perform the tasks required of one in the pursuit of one's chosen job and or career. As capital therefore, and as is parallel to other such as fixed capital, it becomes legitimate within the situation of the investment in one's human self, and as capital, to seek to obtain best of monetary and material return on one's investment. This material reward is then shown and seen in a highly materialistic life style, which then establish and create self worth in individuals. When material returns becomes the main factor that reflects the value of human beings and as they are seen as human capital, and where there are persons who have low levels of education with little or no skills or training, and are not able to distinguish one's self and self worth in the possession and display of materials, such persons come quickly to a feeling of alienation. In such a situation means such as crime and violence is pursued to obtain these materials to provide self worth, not only to be seen as fit, but even to be seen as the fittest.

Within the frame of this vector of social behaviour we arrive at a situation where there is an absence of the spirituality in which a morality of usefulness can arise. When personal material well being is the dominant force in survival and not responsibility towards anyone in society in general out of which flows the morality of being useful, dishonourable and criminal actions becomes a rational endeavour. When these actions are pursued with force and might as is legitimate within the context of the survival of the fittest, we move towards the deconstructing of society as being a civilized place. When within the movement towards this deconstruction, which will be evidenced then by high level of fear that each has for others and endeavours constantly increase to make one feel secure and safe, and more emphasis is given to rights and forbearance than to responsibility and usefulness, society is further weakened, and this then hastens its deconstruct as a civilized place.

In all societies we will find there persons seeking not rights but to be responsible and accordingly useful in the giving of service there and by so doing satisfying primarily, the spiritual dimension of their humanity. One frame within which they seek to serve the people and society is that of seeking to be part of the governance of the state. This is where policies of state organizations are developed and managed, and where too the law and order and subsequent rules and regulations within which we live our daily life, is established. The spirituality of these laws that provides the rules and regulations and in which our lives are determined, also determines and defines ultimately our spirituality, our hope, fears, joys and humanity. The other frame in which others consciously seek to give service is through guiding them to a wholly spiritual life within the transcendental, inexplicable and imponderable spirit of God and as is expressed in the theological parameter of a religion; that which provides to the human beings where they find themselves in this diverse world harmony with all life that they experience in their environment.. Such persons considered religious and or holy, serve the people by providing them with a spirituality within which they live their lives and the determining and defining of their humanity. In the pursuit of service to their fellow human beings through seeking to have them live their lives within a religious frame, these persons and some of those who have accepted wholly the guidance given, are some times said to live outside of the realities of their society, and in this manner become dysfunctional citizens, as they seek more to serve God more than the serving of man through the connect to God. In this then their usefulness to man in society is diminished. In the case of the persons who seek to serve their fellow human beings through service in the governance of the state, their usefulness to the people in society, though somewhat removed, does not become such as those who seek to do so within a religious frame, both of whom impact on the humanity and spirituality of the people therein.

The spirituality of usefulness that arises where an individual serves another in their everyday existence, and in this acknowledging that our humanity is derived from our collective human situation arising from the collective impact of their actions, escapes the vast majority of human beings in societies. It is the collective spirituality of usefulness and its impact that fosters and creates a civilized society. This spirituality of usefulness in the creating and the enhancing of the material well being of one's fellow human beings through individual and group relationships, and which is usually considered business is not a dominant feature in society. It is what is obtained from such actions and endeavours that are dominant and important. In this manner therefore, it embraces the mantra of the survival of the fittest which determines a consequential humanity and spirituality from which the might is right morality is derived, and the proclamation and acclamation is such becomes more important than any concern with responsibility.

Usefulness at the individual and group level lends itself to collaborative and creative endeavours that determine a civilized spirituality and humanity and where the survival of the fit provides the basis for our relationships, in what then becomes a civilized community. When usefulness in discharge of responsibility becomes the dominant basis for our relationships the consequential behaviour of human beings in society therefore will be to seek opportunities in all the things they do to serve their fellow human beings in enhancing their material and spiritual well being and by so doing the society. In being useful one serves one's own self as one serves others.

Usefulness and production relations

A pervasive concept and concern of Karl Marx (1818 – 1883) of Germany was the matter of production relations in the western and European capitalist societies and as he experienced then. Earlier, Adam Smith (1723 – 1790) of Great Britain, in his writing "Wealth of Nations" provided Europe, with the concept of division of labour in the real production sector in particular, for the enabling of increased productivity. This was pursued and indeed productivity and production did increase, and it became a major determining factor in this sector of industry and business. It was not the workers in general in what then became factories, that benefited, and persons who were artisans where they were in earlier times, but the owners of these new workshops, being then called factories, and as they are now known today. These factory workers then who a few decades or so earlier would have been artisans in their own workshops became known as the proletariat and working class at the time of Karl Marx writing, and the owners of the workshops that were transformed into factories, capitalists. He saw what he then identified as production relationships in the situation where the considered working class people were doing jobs that were very simple and repetitive and which required the minimum of their human and in particular their mental self, and the owners of these factories, the capitalists, how they pursued their lives in society. He spoke of the evolution from the earlier feudal times of the upper classes to that of the landed gentry and capitalists, and the lower classes that were then, the proletariat and workers in factories. Marx said that this situation where the concept of co-determination in business organization was becoming part of the law and order of society there, that it would evolve further into what would then be a communal situation. The concept of communal production relationships was transformed within a number of western societies, to one of a communist state which became then responsible totally, not for setting the parameters for how each served the other in society, but for doing so themselves even to that of the determining of the daily material well being of the people. The determining within a law and order frame of how individuals could express the collaborative and collective responsibility dimension of their individual humanity in their relationships was not embraced, as much as the power that came to the persons that served in the governance of the state, for their own well being. Within the governance of the state was to be found, those that were the fittest, and paradoxically so, the fit.

Communal production, which evolved into communist states in the western societies which have the spirituality of the survival of the fittest as a major vector in their humanity have fallen apart. The spirituality of the survival of the fit allows more for collective and collaborative relationships wherein usefulness of an individual can be seen. Societies that have a culture in which this type of relationship is the dominant the one, there is an evolving of communal production, which has led to an enhanced human development and material well being there.

Marx spoke of three dimensions in respect of alienation; firstly, that of the labourer from their labour and which was reflected in the considered inequitable reward for this as was reflected in their monetary returns they received for this in the form of wages, and as against that which was obtained from the persons who purchased the goods they received and the amount of this which went to the owners of these factories; the capitalists; as profits. The second dimension was that of the worker from them self, as in that they did not seem to them self as having meaning and purpose in life, as the tasks given to them to perform within Adam Smith's organizational concept of the division of labour, required little or no mental effort for most of the people in the organization. The third dimension was that of themselves as labourers and they within the frame of being depersonalized as human capital and being the least valuable of such, consequentially not having much worth in society. In earlier times, these people who had now become labourers were artisans in workshops, and the products of these places could be seen all around them in the communities in which they lived. In this situation they as individuals considered them self responsible and useful persons and too, their community; society. This connection, gave to their lives, meaning and purpose.

These two latter forms of alienation, the disconnection of the individual from their society, is pervasive in our western societies of today, where it is not only amongst the labouring class within the real production sector; the term real being that which is material, touchable, concrete, that which is now considered the productive sector ; but also within the services production sector. One finds in this sector such professions as teachers, doctors, lawyers, bankers, financial advisers, journalists and persons serving in the governance of the state. Implicit in the concept and logic of a productive sector is that of sectors and persons serving there that are not in fact productive members of our society. Going further within that logic, institutions and organizations such as schools, colleges, universities, hospitals, health clinics, banks, newspapers, the police force all these bodies and the people of society serving there would be considered not essential to society for a good quality of life there. In considering the real production sector as the productive sector unwittingly precedence is given to the material dimension of our humanity rather than it being connected to the mental and spiritual dimension of our selves. The reality is that in respect of teachers who are the identifiable persons in educating and the imparting of a morality and value system to the children of society, who then become adults there, when we note the decline of good and the increase of bad behaviour in society, we see in this negative production. In respect of doctors who are highly identifiable persons in the physical health and care of people in society, when we see the life span of people there lengthening, in this we see positive production. It is the alienation of so many of our citizens in society, both in the real production sector and the services production sector where the material dimension of our selves is seen as more important than the spiritual dimension and disconnected from it that we find the display of materials becoming the measure of one's self worth.

Production relations and production occurs in all our human relationships in the production of either goods or services. It is out of these production relations and relationships that we create business and where we as individuals, for most of us, find usefulness and meaning in our life. In the identifying of people in society, wittingly or unwittingly, as implicitly not being productive and accordingly not useful, the ground is created for their alienation and also for a struggle amongst then to establish their self worth, all this now within the morality and value system of the survival of the fittest. In this struggle where sophist argumentation is also a tool; and as used by our considered intelligentsia; and we use this term to identify those who are generally the ones that serve in the educating of the people in society and also those that steal from others, we demean and diminish these former persons, as too our society. The first of these people, the teachers, doctors etc, produce a constructive and positive spiritual force, and the second, those that steal, a negative and destructive one. This occurs when our physical self is disconnected from the spiritual one and where our physical and material self identifies us and the survival of this self as the fittest, not the fit, becomes our value system and morality by default.

The spirituality of usefulness which first of all gives meaning to one's life and then expresses itself in self worth and pride without the need for excessive display of materials and too, in the connection to one's fellow human being, is the converse of the disconnection and alienation which is usual and general today and can be seen mostly in the larger metropolitan communities. This alienation in a passive form is one in which the individual sees and feels no bonds and connection between themselves and society in general, and pursue their own interests above that of others and society, within the context and pre-eminence of human rights rather than that of civil rights. The active form of this alienation is seen in the mayhem of violence, some of this violence being the environmental degradation that is engendered in the pursuit of one's material well being, and in the manner of the disposal of one's garbage; and also in the use of drugs for hallucinating, this now being considered for the most part as medicinal purpose.

At the recognition and acceptance that all our relations and relationships are productive either of a material or a spiritual well being and needs in society and within which we make a contribution there the ground will be laid for many more persons to be considered as being useful and responsible citizens leading to self worth. In this we reduce the propensity for alienation while we increase and widen the sphere to serve our fellow human beings and thereby and provide the ground for entrepreneurship and enterprise, where we do so in the form of business. The struggle for being the fittest and this within the frame of one's human self and rights which leads ultimately to alienation and disconnection from society and a dysfunctional humanity by default, will be replaced with a humanity of self worth that is engendered which comes from being useful, and in serving others in society. When we do this in business in the producing of soap or security, potatoes and peace, envelopes and education, ginger and governance, we enrich our lives as we enrich society.

Usefulness and the increase of choice

In the inexorable reductive spirituality that is implicit within the framework of thought of the survival of what is considered the fittest, choice is reduced. However within that of the survival of the fit as is seen in the grandeur of the diversity of nature, choice is increased. The conduct of business, trade and industry between persons, communities and nations has generally been in the context of the survival of the fittest and of the general exploitation of this transactional relation and situation leading to the exploitation of others and to their diminishing. The essence of the conduct of such affairs where the western culture is dominant is reflected in the mantra there, that "business is business "and accordingly, not a part of the social relations that it is considered to be in some cultures. The consequence of the diminishing of the other party with whom one conducts business particularly so in the matter of trade is that it reduces the supply of goods and services, usually first in the quality of the supplies, and later in the quantity. After this, relationships deteriorate and become adversarial. These adversarial relationships can become open conflicts, and where this situation exists between communities or nations, it leads to war. This adversarial relationship occurs too, not only between the parties trading, but others seeking to dominate and capture sources of supply to satisfy their needs and choice. What we find here is this domination either through slavery, bondage, or inequitable trade, affects the continuity of the choice that is provided in this manner as a consequence of the diminishing and impoverishment of the other.

When choice is provided or obtained in the situation of equity which flows from that of the survival of the fit, rather than that of the fittest, and where each party in this relationship is consequently served, the well being and quality of life for each party is enriched and the situation becomes a sustainable one. We see here that the impoverishment of others leads to our own impoverishment, part of which is the concern that must be given to the safety of our selves. Anxiety which creates fear is engendered in these relationships, individuals against individuals, communities against communities, nations against nations and we then use iron to make guns which we can use to destroy each other and in order to protect and give ourselves a sense of security, rather than to make ploughs that can help us to grow food to feed each other. Where we enrich each other in the process of providing choice, our humanity and our existence become enhanced, beginning from our near community of individuals to the far one of nations and the world.

2.2. Serving in society through business.
Entrepreneurship and enterprise

In the pursuit of being useful there are individuals that ask themselves what are the needs of one's fellow human beings, what are one's skills and talents, and then uses these as best as one is able to serve the people as best as one can. There are those who seek to be employed by others and in a situation of security and others considered entrepreneurs who seek to create a business enterprise for the purpose of serving others. In seeking to satisfy the needs of one's fellow human beings within an enterprise that they then seek to create, they must then seek to obtain such material resources as are necessary for this purpose, and in their pursuit of being useful. In all of these endeavours one is rewarded as they contribute to society.

The individual who seeks to create a new enterprise is considered an entrepreneur, and it is usual that this person conceptualizes a new product, or the modification of one, in this their pursuit of usefulness. Such persons, in their entrepreneurial endeavours in pursuit of seeking to serve society, take risks that others who seek to be useful, do not take. This then is not asking for rights and forbearance in order to serve or exist as one wish whilst at the same time reducing the life space of others and the general diminishing of the well being that then exists. It is first the enhancement of society through one's contribution, thereby establishing the ground and capacity for society to give to one greater reward, and in an equitable manner for one's usefulness.

The entrepreneur then, is one who seeks to be useful and who creates a new enterprise in which they use their talents and creatively in serving society whilst accepting risks that are involved in such situations. This spirituality and humanity is more one that is nurtured than taught, even if one teaches the conduct of a business enterprise, to an entrepreneur, whose enterprise usually begins as a small one. This spirituality and humanity of entrepreneurship is derived from the confluence of societal forces of one's community, family, friends and role models which converges in and energizes the individual who then in this frame pursues the task of being useful. The entrepreneur will more be taught how to conduct the affairs of business that will allow then the continuity that they would wish in their affairs of business and of usefulness in society. The entrepreneur is served as they seek to serve in a business enterprise.

Enterprise and management

Entrepreneurship can be considered the spirit of adventure in usefulness and the pursuit of service to one's fellow human beings through the vehicle of a new business for the provision of goods and services, perhaps a combination of both in a manner that provides in the context of our society, good value for money, and for which people will seek one out. In the action of providing within a business enterprise goods and services to one's fellow human beings, through offering then choice in the satisfying of their needs, one then enhances the quality of their lives. This is done through the arrangement of, and systems of information and knowledge, equipment, finance and capital, and collective human endeavour that is called labour, and come to what is called administration and management of the business enterprise In the pursuit of the goals of the enterprise which is essentially that of service by an individual or group of individuals to others in society in the satisfaction of their material well being, we find risks, the least being, that individuals cannot forecast all the consequences of their actions and in fact has limitations even in their knowingness and knowledge.

There are things that fall outside the conception and perception of human beings that impact upon their being in the pursuit of their daily existence some of which are dysfunctional and deleterious, some benign, others extremely useful and are called miracles. One seeks at all times to minimize the deleterious and the dysfunctional. We would hardly refuse to act in the contemplation of the reality of our ultimate not-knowingness and the uncertainties of our today and tomorrows and it is in this that we find management, seeking to make things occur in the manner that we wish them to. A measure and the effectiveness of management therefore, is the extent to which things happen is what was wished and desired. In the process of management the most critical dimension is that of the human one, that of those with whom we work to serve others, and those whom we seek to serve. Those with whom we work have their skills and competencies, their values and attitudes as expressed in their humanity; and those whom we wish to serve have their values and attitudes, and consequential humanity as is expressed in their needs and desires. The commonality here is our values and attitudes these being the essence of our humanity, determined in the relationships first by the society in general and then within our near community in which we work together in serving, and too by whom we serve.

The value system which allows firstly for a debt of gratitude to society for our humanity and therefore one to accept responsibility for the continuity of society, allows too the use of one's spiritual and psychic energies, and material resources in the managing of affairs of the business and enterprise in a manner such that its hallmark will not be that of exploitation and the diminishing of others in society within the mores of the survival of the fittest. It will move in the direction of the survival of the fit, where all in society are enhanced in these relationships of serving and being served. It is more within the mores and values of the survival of the fit that entrepreneurship is facilitated than that of the survival of the fittest.

Enterprise and business

An enterprise is a structure of relationships of persons who seek to serve their fellow human beings in society through the provision to them of some goods and services and through which these persons within the structure obtains their rewards which enables and facilitates them their existence in society. A business enterprise can be one where all the resources required for it is wholly provided by to those who operate and work within it, or one where others outside of its daily operations, provide to this business either, or both material and intellectual support. Reward for those who serve in a business organization or is served by it, is generally a material and monetary one, and rests upon an agreed upon arrangement. Within the context of usefulness and serving society, such monetary reward becomes a transaction of equity, rather than one of exploitation. Business transactions in this manner acknowledges that equity allows for the continuity of relationships through the survival and enhancement of both parties to the relationships, whereas in an exploitative one, one party in the relationship is diminished and accordingly over time the relationship will come to an end.

The manner in which we perceive and conduct business is reflected in the manner in which we use the word. When one say's that one is minding one's business it speaks to the idea that one is dealing with a situation that is very personal and which usually no other, at least not the other party being spoken to should seek to become involved. There can also be at times the suggestion that the person to whom one is speaking should be concerned about that person's own affairs and should not seek to be concerned with the affairs of the other. When one says that one is looking after one's business the situation is somewhat different. There is the understanding here that the matter that is being dealt with, perhaps within an enterprise, are those through which one obtains one's livelihood, the material needs for sustenance in society. In minding one's business, one is dealing with what is private and personal in one's life and existence, whilst in looking after one's business, one is dealing with what provides the material sustenance of one's existence.

Another usage which provides another perspective of business, is seen in the statement to someone during some social interaction that "this is business", or in identifying to others that a human and social interaction was such. It is to be understood that the party was highly focused and dispassionate in the interaction in seeking to secure for themselves the maximum material benefit and advantage in the situation. Business therefore can be seen as a transactional relationship given to the material things of life rather than a spiritual one, at both levels of a private and personal one, and also as a public one. These two dimensions of our human existence, the material and the spiritual, are generally separated from each other, for many in our society, one disconnected from the other. It is not seen that our whole life and interactions are connected and have to do with business, that of our existing, and which for many of us now in this world do at the most basic level in the continuing of endeavour for the whole of their life of seeking to secure for themselves food, clothes and shelter. In all of these endeavours by people in society, there are those who fail in this goal in their life. There are others however who give no concern to such things for themselves, but do so for the others that have failed to do so for themselves, considering that if one serves these others, one becomes useful, and is served through the will of God. Essentially, one is useful and is rewarded; one's existence justified and one then becomes fit to serve.

Such persons who in their humanity prioritize their spiritual self above their physical one can be found in many fields of endeavours, where they dedicate their whole lives to the service of others and without any concern for a regular and a considered equitable reward in the payment of a wage or salary or fees for their services. They serve without counting the cost to themselves and seek only the basic material needs which enables them to continue in service to their fellow human beings. These persons for the most part place themselves in bondage of service to others, this therefore their business; one that is spiritually motivated rather materially so. Business construed as the activity of human beings in the pursuit of securing one's existence in society, is found in organizations created by citizens for this purpose, and also by the state. In the situation of gratefulness for one's humanity and in the spirituality of seeking to serve our fellow human beings, rather than to receive from them, we can do this alone or in collaboration with others, and this then becomes one's business which we then identify as a private sector organization, and such is usually considered a charitable one. We do business of this nature in organizations created by the state, where we serve the society in general in the providing of services to them that is generally considered as impacting on the general quality of life for all, and identify such business organizations as public sector organizations. How we serve in these organizations rests ultimately on the pursuit of responsibility to our fellow human beings, and consequential service to them, rather than that of rights and forbearance. In the pursuit of business within private or public sector organizations, and within the framework of responsibility and usefulness, we contribute to the creating of a sustainable human condition in our world.

Dysfunction in serving in business

Very few persons are able to provide for themselves all that is required for their existence, and this is the ground for business and trade, and in earlier times the basis for many wars. In the past the first reliance and source of supplement of our needs was our complement of nature, the opposite sex, with whom one created new life and the continuity of human kind. It was general that the female of the specie who in the nurturing of the new life had to be essentially sedentary, to perform other tasks that in that situation could be done and which would enhance the live and relationships of these persons. Out of this grew a division of labour, where females performed household and domestic tasks, and the males, the hunter, gatherer, trader, warrior; fighting for things he desired for his household but did not produce, that being an option for the acquiring of things. It was in this the fighting for things for one's survival where the physical dimension of human beings was a determining factor that the ground was laid for the later concept of the survival of the fittest.

The concept of the division of labour was seen in the tasks that were done in households and Adam Smith in his book "Wealth of nations" extended the concept in the performance of tasks that were required in the making of goods that people required in their lives then, and which Marx called "production relations". Frederick W. Taylor (1856 – 1915) of USA extended this concept of division of labour further in his book "Scientific Management" and all these ideas contributed to increased productivity in the business organizations that produced for the most part goods, all of this increasing its totality in society, and the material well being there. In the past the provision and acquisition of food and a house, this structure then becoming our home which we shared with our family, and where our humanity is nurtured and mostly determined, was a major endeavour for our survival. Today for many, our humanity with its need for instant satisfaction and gratification, we see this for the most part, being satisfied within a fast food environment. As we spend less time in search for our material survival and existence as we have much more available to us, we spend more time in the spiritual frame of our existence, not in churches or such religious places, but with likeminded persons in places usually in what then becomes places of entertainment and recreation, physically and spiritually.

The story has been told of a man who became a hermit as he would be rid of this modern society, and went therefore to live in the forests. He could however be pointed out at least once per year in the village that was close to the forest where he came to sell very cheaply the berries that grew in the forest and which he had reaped, to obtain for himself such things as toilet paper, salt and wash rags. It is found here that marginal though this was, the hermit was still connected to the village and the society, as human life and existence is such that few if any one person is able to provide for themselves all that they need and would wish for in the living of their daily life. Consequential to this and our living together, we become the human beings that we are. It may well be considered by many that the hermit's type of existence did not provide for the freedom of spirit and humanity that occurs where one lives fully within a community, be that of a family, clan, tribe, or village or nation.

It may well be that the hermit who spent his time in and amongst the trees and the birds, the blossoms and the flowers, experiencing at very close range the changes and the seasonal form of nature that he found there, had within him a humanity and spirituality that is far different from one that is engendered in a fast food environment. His spirituality and humanity would be likely to be one that allows him to take plenty of time in the preparing of his meals as he found enjoyment in the act, and then in the eating of the different and contrasting tastes of the food that he found there in the forest. As the hermit did, and as some of us do, when we look around us we see quite a few species of life in the plants and animals with whom we co-exist and which deepens our human condition. In this we find and appreciate diversity which makes us begin to think of our survival, not as the fittest, but as the fit. It could be said that the hermit's existence impacted very little on this world of diversity; the forests, the animal life there, and the village to which he was close and to which he supplied his berries. He was however, marginal though it might have been, useful in providing choice to the people of the village, and contributing to their lives.

In the context of the survival of the fit, in business, one's usefulness is more determined by one's self and emanates from the desire to serve and to be useful in the enhancement of humanity in general and within the frame of one's own humanity. The example of this has been persons that have dedicated their lives to the service of others by placing themselves almost in bondage to society in their endeavours. We find this in some religious bodies and institutions in society where people serve, not in the promotion of their religion, but in service to their fellow human beings there in the satisfying of their material needs.

Paradoxically so, society moves on to the path of the demeaning of its citizens and being dysfunctional when it is so that only persons who have dedicated their lives to assist those who through an aberrant physical or spiritual humanity in life and living are not able to do so, and must be helped and served by these persons so dedicated to serve. Within the logic of the survival of the fittest, the physically dysfunctional and aberrant when it becomes the task of others to serve them, these persons who serve then can be seen as persons themselves not able to serve and be useful to others in the mainstream of society. Where the aberration of the person's humanity is more a spiritual one, and they are served more so than others, particularly so in the providing to them their material needs for existence without concern for the development of this spiritual dimension and humanity, this then makes such aberrations more valuable than that which enables one to contribute to society. We find in this, two vectors of dysfunctions, one that impacts upon those that seek to serve and another on those that are served.

It is in this we find the need for rules and regulations arising from the law and order that is created by our governors for the governance of the state, to guide us in the conduct of all these affairs and inter relationships in our human endeavours in society to be useful and to serve each. Where society in general seek to be useful in the serving in the uplifting of its citizens, both spiritually and materially, without a disconnect from each, we find in this a shared responsibility and the deepening of usefulness of individuals there, each to the other, and so too, those who would spend their lives serving those lesser of us.

2.3. Serving in society in state governance
State governance

We are born in this human world society into our family, community and nation. Most of us experience our world, first through our family, then our community and then our nation. The nation state is for us that which sets the ultimate parameters within which our material and spiritual well being is determined and satisfied. A materialist and humanist perspective on how one experience's the world, and how we behave in it therefore is that the relationships which surrounds our pursuit of obtaining our material well being, survival, existence herein, is the dominant and determining factor of our humanity and consequential behaviour. This perspective allows us to recognize that we can alter and determine our own selves.

Within the latter half of this recently past century there were had states that sought consciously to determine their own selves and humanity then, and changes were made in the manner and structure in which they governed themselves. It was sought through this change to impact on the consequential relationships of the people in the state in the pursuit of their material well being, these being considered production relations and that this change would extend to the impacting upon the spirituality and the determining of the humanity of the people therein. It was accepted that the value system within which state governance was pursued was that which determined the rules and regulations within which we obtained our material sustenance and existence, and ultimately then, our humanity in society. In this we see then that the behaviour and character of the governors, in the governance of the state within such structures as they exist then was a major contributing factor in the determining of the humanity of people in society.

The new structure of state governance, the influencing and determining of behaviour of human beings in society, had within it people whose existence was within the value system of the survival of the fittest, where might is right, and this new system fell apart, governance returned, essentially to what it was before, and for which the people were familiar. New structures of governance are meaningful and become more valuable where it is recognized that new values and attitudes are required for its functioning, and where too it deepens this spirituality and morality in its continuity.

Where there is a governance structure that facilitates and engenders in all persons who serve within it a positive spirituality of usefulness and it reflects there the humanity of the survival of the fit, it is then that there will be a movement from the pervasive and embedded in our humanity at an unconscious manner, the spirituality of the survival of the fittest.

Governance and serving

For the most part, we as human beings are born into our human family and experiences and exist there, within the mores and values and culture of their state and community, from which their humanity flows. One experiences and learns the impact of the state and community; positively or negatively. At times one experiences the negative aspect so deeply, that one seeks to set one's self outside of these prevailing mores and values and to change or destroy it, and so does. Out of such changes the lives of many people of the society are enhanced and here we have a positive consequence. There are times however when such changes benefits them or a group of few others, but for the most part, others are diminished. In this we experience a negative consequence.

Jamaica had a slave structure society and this was destroyed by the slaves. Within this slave society one is aware that there were slaves there for whom life was well enough within the system as they had there roles which allowed them rewards which gave them a sense of self worth, above that which was general amongst the slaves, and generally fellow Africans. In all societies there are those who live well enough in it and benefit from its structure, and there are those who do not, and for whom life is short and brutish, and as it was for many in our past Jamaican slave society. There is an agony, anguish and dilemma in life and giving service to one's fellow human beings through the destroying of a structure of governance and replacing it with another in which more persons will benefit, but where in the destroying of the first, human lives and their condition is diminished. There are those who experience the state in a positive manner, seek to be part of it even to improve upon it for themselves, and even for others. One comes to the service in the governance of the state and the improving of society from either of these experiences and consequential perspective. A truly civilized society and state is one in which all human beings there, live their lives for the most part in peace and harmony and without fear of each other and as they seek to be responsible and useful citizens.

In being useful in the governance of the state, one can come to this from that of seeking to make it one in which more of the people in general lead better lives, or for a few others. One does so within some moral frame and or perspective, and when this is done within the underlying spirituality of the survival of the fittest, adversarial and confrontational relationships are engendered. When it is done within the spirituality of the survival of the fit, creative tensions are engendered as it allows too for collaborative relationships from which innovation obtains.

Dysfunctions in serving in governance

The concept of the survival of the fittest is as the concept of the survival of the fit, deleterious when taken to the extreme. The survival of the fittest provides us with the legitimacy of might being right which has allowed for slavery and the holding of others in bondage to the mighty. It provided too for apartheid in one society and in another for the creating of a caste; a group of people; considered untouchables. Within this context, it is the fittest and or group of those citizens so considered the fittest that determines the usefulness of individuals, with the state governors being part of this determination through the parameters of the rules and regulation, law and order that they establish and within which the people live their life. These considered fittest persons and dominant social force create and determine the parameters within which we live our lives, and do so too, in respect of one's usefulness in society. This is done without much concern for the individuality and humanity of the people in general. It is in this context that those who hold state power offer rights to all in order to alleviate and reduce the dysfunctions that occur in the life of people there. It is in this that rights becomes more considered than responsibility, although the latter is the source out of which usefulness and the consequential search to give service to one's fellow human beings generally arise.

Some societies in the past considered it best that persons who served in the governance of the state, should do so removed from the general social space of their society, and even from their families, and so this was done. It was considered then that these persons would be able to serve the whole society with the highest level of integrity and objectivity. In the removal of such individuals from the general population of society one creates an elite group, and one which begins to lose sensitivity to the everyday experiences of the people and for whom they must determine the parameters of existence. Accordingly some of these parameters may well be flawed. It may well be too that they may not be seen as flawed in the long term but that in the immediate situation such beneficence as occurs to individuals now is reduced and the foregoing of this for the enhancement of the society later, creates a human dilemma.

In adversarial relationships this dilemma is construed as a negative and the ground for conflict, whereas in collaborative relationships where one seeks to be useful, this negative situation and dysfunction becomes one where creative tensions are engendered in the seeking of solutions and the enhancement of the situation.

When one seeks to serve in societies of today and within the underlying value system that is there of the survival of the fittest, one seeks and secures the role of service in governance at the individual level through adversarial social relationships to some and to others, patronage. When such activities are rewarded with what is considered the most worthy of service to one's fellow human beings, that of serving in governance where the parameters of the lives of the citizens in society are determined, it first of all engenders within the state a culture of such behaviour as it also determines the responses of the state to other states. It is considered that if one offers one's self to give service in the governance of the state and within the context of the survival of the fit, it will at the individual level engender there collaborative and complementary relationships. This can however extend to the point where behaviour becomes highly conformal and this being affirmed in the process of governance, and where there will be then, a reduction of creativity in thinking and ideas amongst these persons who seek to serve society. A state that is collaborative and complementary in its relationships with another is very likely to respond less aggressively and more creatively and constructively to these other states in their relationships. The survival of the fittest provides us with the logic of the inexorable movement by might the diminishing and deconstruction of diversity and towards that one thing which is considered to be the fittest, with the ultimate determining factor of this being might.

Within the logic of the survival of the fit, when taken to its extreme it brings us to aberrations that are less deleterious and dysfunctional than that of the survival of the fittest, which provides the ground for individualism and the domination of one over the other. The survival of the fit provides us with the logic of the entertaining of diversity and the accommodating of this out of which we select and determine how we will be guided in our existence, this within the recognition and acknowledgement of a transcendental, imponderable and inexplicable force that is identified as the spirit of God, and too, which we experience differently in our diverse universe. The dysfunctions are seen as high levels of passivity and low levels of creativity.

The survival of the fittest takes us to rights and forbearance where paradoxically tolerance of all is considered that which is right. In this situation where tolerance is right the question arises as to how one treats with intolerance, as that too must be tolerated. The survival of the fit takes us to responsibility and usefulness through service and within which there is civil rights and what is considered right.

Thoughts on the western structure and system of governance

The structures and systems of state governance, which for the most part determines the behaviour of the persons that are actively engaged within the process, reflects the norms and values that are operative then in society, as also the spiritual superstructure of its culture and the mores and values within this. In most of the states of the world there is practiced there in the governance of their nation state what is considered democracy, and accordingly identified as a democratic nation. In the western societies democracy exists within the system of thought of the survival of the fittest, where in the process of seeking to obtain the opportunity to give service in the governing of the state, and as the people's representative, to be involved in the process of the determining of policies for state organizations and then in the determining of the law and order for society, the individual seeking to do so becomes first engaged in a struggle to do so. This opportunity when obtained by being the fittest provides the legitimacy for this winner in the struggle to act as they see fit in the process of governance and within the mantra of the winner taking all.

There are two structures for the governance of a state in a democratic manner that are highly favoured, one that is called the Westminster model and as is found in England (UK), and the other, the Presidential model, as is found in the United States of America (USA). In the western world, the Communist model of democratic governance of the state gave the illusion of not having winners and being the survival of the fit. In reality there were cliques to the right and to the left, which struggled for ascendancy within its structure and process, and at the obtaining of such and considered winners, there was a purge of the other as is legitimate in the concept of the winner taking all. The Westminster and the Presidential models have displayed greater longevity than the communist variation of democracy, as within these structures and systems, mechanisms have been developed to reduce many of the deleterious and dysfunctional occurrences which arises where the winner takes all the power and authority of the state in the determining of society at both the individual and collective level.

State governance can be considered to have two main dimensions. Firstly we have the organizational mechanisms used in the process of governance and considered here as the structure of governance. Secondly, there is the substance of governance which is the matter of the formation and implementation of policies that guides the undertaking of government and how we as citizens of the state relate to each other in life and living together there. From earlier times we had families consisting of persons that were biologically intertwined, and next in the extending of our social space, clans or tribes, ethnic groups communities and our nation that was led by such persons as warriors, chiefs, clan leaders, and kings, all of which derived their leadership role of governance from the exercise of what was considered more might than the combination of such with the spirituality that came from their mental and spiritual self. It was within the dimension of might that a leadership role was given and made legitimate and by which it was maintained.

The spirituality of care and concern for one's family that engendered activities of hunting, and fighting others for doing so, which then extended to others in one's social space. In the frame of the survival of the fittest, the hunter became the warrior, then the chief and later the king and monarch of all one surveyed. In some nations of today the inherited state governance power that the monarch wielded has been transferred to the people through the exercise of collective might that arose from individual right. The organizational mechanisms for the enabling of the people to govern themselves designed within the system of thought of the survival of he fittest, has brought us to what we today accept as democracy, where the people of a state nation select the governors of their state. This expression of the voice of the people, in many instances strident in populism and not of reasoned thought, is said to be the voice of God. In a number of states the voice of the people as being the voice of God is eschewed, and it is considered that God speaks to a few, his clerics, and that people power as is said to exist in democracies is blasphemy. State power and governance is therefore for these few chosen men of God. It is considered here, that God governs rather than the people, but through the human beings who have sought and received the wisdom of God and his blessing, rather than the seeking and receiving the blessing of their fellow human beings. These persons of God, the Clerics, then govern by the laws and postulates of God which reposes in their religion and comes to us through some miraculous and revelatory event of a human being, then considered a human agent of God, such as Jesus Christ considered as the son of God, and from which Christianity comes.

From within our western and Christian societies we have had Plato, who lived here on earth in the Greek City states, before the coming of Christ, who led us to democracy. In his city states then, he saw philosopher kings, today's academicians or scholars as being the persons from whom those who would govern these city states then should be selected, as he considered them the cadre of the best of persons for this task. In this we find that in the structure and system of governance the quality of persons there, those who are fit, is of importance, and as is seen too where the Clerics in other states are considered there as being the ones that are fit to do so. Such persons as were considered had within them the knowledge, wisdom and character of the highest level that would provide to the state, the highest level of governance. Within the past five hundred years, western societies have actively sought to have a clear delineation and separation of the governance of the state and society, from religious and clerical matters. This link remains in some societies however, but in many of these there are societal tensions for the separation of these matters as it now generally exists in the western world. It is considered that state governance must go beyond the dictates of God as is experienced and perceived in the past history of human beings, which is not in keeping with our modern knowledge and realities and what may even be considered new expressions of God. In the governance of the state one must seek to enhance the condition of all the people therein, and not only of one group of persons; sect or religion; over others, and this without the diminishing of others.

When governance of the state resides in the context of individuals serving fellow human beings in society, it becomes more likely to enhance each citizen's life in society. This is even further enhanced when the governors listen to their fellow human beings there and to their knowledge as is to be found generally in the people of society of today, rather than as it was in earlier times when it was found in select and identifiable groups, such as philosopher-kings and the clerics. In this manner we make the democratic governance process relevant to the society as it has evolved over time, and into one that is more participatory as it was intended to be when it was first considered by Plato, rather than the representative one that exists now in the frame and context of the survival of the fittest. When in governance we listen to each other in a discourse and accept our not-knowingness and mortality, and as we seek within the perspectives that we hold, to find solutions to resolve problems that we find in our daily lives, it becomes no longer the matter of the survival of the fittest but that of the fit. It will not be one of the might of numbers or of the mighty strident and sophist intellectual argumentation that is right, but that of the survival of the fit where within the frame of knowledge and rational discourse, and a morality of civilized behavior and values which then is the dominant character of human beings in society.

The pervasive system of thought of the survival of the fittest, and in which much of our life is pursued is contradicted by the reality that wherever and whichever ground we stand and look out and around us we find the existence of diversity, much of which we enjoy. We find diversity in the skies above us, diversity in the land on which we stand, diversity in the plant and animal life around us, and even amongst us human beings. Later we experience the diversity of the seasons and of the weather. To the extent that we obtain knowledge of our situation and seek harmony in things, out of which we develop our culture and civilization, in this manner we create more joy and pleasure in our experiences and in our life and living. It is not in the pursuit of seeking to conquer and reduce the diversity that we find around us that allows for our joys and pleasure and even our survival, but to live in and enjoy this diversity. It is not then the matter of the fittest, but that of the fit. In the pursuit of this harmony with nature and within our human society we are able to do so not by seeking forbearance and for rights, but by contributing to the enhancement of the harmony through partaking in the endeavours that are more the norm than the aberrant. Our behaviour then is characterized as being responsible and useful. In seeking to become and on becoming a governor in the pursuit of the governance of the society one becomes even more responsible and useful in this wider and diverse social space of the state in the facilitating of citizens there to enjoy this diversity of our human existence.

Concerns on the present structure and systems of governance

A structure of governance based on the system of thought derived from the morality and consequential spirituality of the survival of the fittest, with mechanism to reduce it's deleterious effects in the state where the quality of life for some, and at times the most of the citizens there will not be very high, will allow it to last for a while longer without it falling into decadence. This decadence of civil order will sooner or later be seen and experienced in the level of corruption within the governing class and or elite, and the life span of the organizational mechanisms for corrections of such dysfunctions, becoming shorter and shorter. It will also be expressed in the increasing levels of fear of individuals for their neighbours and where each person seeks to establish security for them self, within the context of rights and forbearance. In this too the tool of sophist argumentation is used in making rights and forbearance of individuals and groups in society as being more important than responsibility and usefulness. All these behaviours move more towards the diminishing of the quality of life for the people in society, than its enhancing. This is what is being found in the western societies, Jamaica in the Caribbean being part of this western world. We live in a world in which it is said that the western cultures are given to individualism and that might is right, the eastern cultures to collaborative collectivism and conformism, the north to a rationalism, objectivity, and passiveness, the south to emotionalism, subjectivity and a general vibrancy of self. The Caribbean is now peopled predominantly by the descendants of those originating from the southern cultures and with this vibrancy of life and living they exist within the western mantra and spirituality of the survival of the fittest, and which then moves the situation of their existence more quickly towards being deleterious and dysfunctional.

The rationale of the survival of the fittest with its logic of an inexorable reductionism and the creating of an atmosphere for the demeaning, diminishing and destruction of others brings with it the alleviation of the dysfunctions that it engenders the reactive corrective mechanism of rights. This then lays the ground further for individualism, and a generally deeper and wider disconnect of an individual from the mainstream of society, and consequently endeavours to enable its enhancement. In this social environment the role model in governance is the identifiable strongman and or charismatic leader and all that this characterizes, part of which is the capacity for confrontation and the diminishing of others. Such strongmen are to be seen too in state enterprises and in private sector business enterprises where they are euphemistically called Czars, and there the total control and direction rests in reality, in this one person's hands. In many cases this leads to faulty direction and miss-management at least, and corruption at worst in their organization, much of this being the result of unidimensional decision making.

The survival of the fit has the logic of collaboration and collectivism and brings with it the corrective mechanism of responsibility which is first expressed in the rule of the group which when it becomes dysfunctional and deleterious is reflected in the suppression of the talent and creativity of individuals therein and moves towards conformist group behaviour. A corrective mechanism can be had within the framework that balances the rewards that are provided, not only for working effectively there, but also for the originating of ideas and the making of such that are put forward useful in the enhancing of the group's endeavours firstly and next that of the well being of society in general which they seek to serve. One's life and existence in society then; one's reward to one's contribution and connection there; rests therefore on the capacity to work with one's fellow human beings collectively for the serving of our fellow human beings, rather than for serving one's self. It brings to it the satisfaction of self worth that arises in the knowledge and reality that in the service with others there is created a general human condition where our survival and situation is enhanced. In this atmosphere it becomes easily recognized that in the survival of the fittest we diminish the social space for our existence, and demean ourselves, whilst we demean and diminish others, but that in being responsible and useful in society by serving our fellow human beings there greater space is had for our existence, and the living of our lives in peace and harmony with each there.

The system of thought based on the survival of the fit allows for the existence of diversity out of which through a collaborative process that is engendered in structures created for this, goes further and enables all persons in this process to be considered fit to survive. Within these parameters and as it has been in the history of human societies, one seeks the best of persons there for the governance of the society. These persons in this process now, who will create the parameters within which we live our lives, will be more given to the listening, hearing and the reference point in the synthesizing of ideas and thoughts for this, rather than the imposing of their will upon others. In earlier times one sought a person, a governor, to represent the people and to act on their behalf. In today's society where the breath and depth of learning of individuals in society is generally greater and wider amongst the people than before, a person is able to more to speak for their own self. This development of individuals moves them more to a participatory democracy, than that of a representative one, and as how it has become. To the extent that this representative democracy is continuingly pursued in the governance of a nation, to that extent that alienation for many will characterize the nation.

Within the logic of the survival of the fittest and the alienation of the citizens there who have learning, formal and informal, activities are pursued by individuals or small groups in which these individuals are visible, and they create then the social space they wish, and which in many cases moves the nation very quickly to the situation of disequilibrium and dysfunction. Many of these actions and activities are pursued within a frame of sophist intellectualism, and spiritualism, for some, and for others, in activities of crime and violence, and where all of this is grounded in a sense of amorality, or of a morality of one's human self over others. This dysfunction is evidenced in the size and the growth of the security service industry; even in societies that are considered developed; that of the protection of individuals and their property. We find there too the concept of overwhelming force and power.

Within the concept and logic of the survival of the fit and where participatory democratic governance exists, alienation is reduced and disequilibrium is generally delayed and not deleterious when it occurs. One finds longer periods of stability wherein which vectors of dysfunctions that causes disequilibrium, outside of those considered natural disasters, can be recognized and action pursued to minimize and correct them. The dominant type of dysfunction coming from the stability and continuity of many vectors in the process of governance is the slowness in the acceptance and use of new ideas in the taking of decisions for initiatives. Nevertheless, these decisions are usually proactive ones and of a high level of effectiveness and when done, high levels of energies are released in the pursuit of usefulness within the frame of a participatory, collective and collaborative endeavour, and where solutions to problems and outcomes are clearly visible and enhancing.

Circular nature of structure and systems

The permeant struggle for being the fittest in order to survive and to have access for our material well being becomes later a pervasive spiritually in our existence and by which we live.

It becomes our value system out of which springs our morality of life and a system of thought which then underlies our governance and its structure. For most of us we are born into this which becomes our humanity, and is considered in general our culture. We accept this for the most part, but from time to time there are those amongst us who question this, how did we become ourselves. For some of us it is the imponderable spirit of God that is beyond us and for others it is that which we find ourselves amongst, the physical world of ours that is diverse. Here we find the simple duality of perspectives, that of the mental leading to a spiritual one, and that of the physical leading to a materialistic one.

In our diverse world and physical environments we create in our daily lives, different rhythms for our existence in each of these and out of which we have a synthesis of thought from out of which we create our governance structures. In our diverse world, one in which there has been a great not-knowingness of others and the universe we created barriers, each of us, that which we knew ourselves and of ourselves; and that which we knew not of others. In our daily lives that which we knew and could prove to others that we knew, even through sophist arguments, such ideas became the mantra of our lives and the determining of who was the fittest to guide, to govern and to rule us. The persons who displayed uncertainty of posited ideas were considered weak, and those who displayed not-knowingness of such, not fit to be heard. For some yesterday and today, it was God that gave them certainty, and for others, the sword of yesterday and today, guns. We are born within these varying structures and systems of governance, and flowing from this our humanity and existence is determined.

Our knowledge today enables us to have a far greater appreciation of ourselves and humanity as we struggle to find the ground to exist with enhanced freedom from fear. We have come to realize that there are two major vectors that guide and direct us and create our humanity. The first major vector is that of governance and in particular its structure, and the second, is that of the knowledge, the spirituality and humanity of the governors as they pursue the tasks of governance. A dimension of this vector is that which we consider knowledge and truth, is sometimes not so. Most of us in the western world know that there was the acceptance as truth and knowledge in times past that the world was flat, not only by the unlearned in society, but also by the learned. We all of us now know that that truth was a lie. We know too, now most of us, that this truth was proven a lie by one considered then to be less than well grounded. This person was willing to take the risk of their truth, sought help in the matter and did obtain this, and today the ancestors of this person are honoured for this action. This action is one which brought the now considered new world to the old world, and now the accepted knowledge that the world is round.

This history allows us to be humble with that which we consider the facts of life and truth as it gives evidence that there is more than one perspective to that which we consider the fact of life and living and our human situation. We can also recognize here that that which we consider the wisdom of the people and as is expressed in their voices and to be that of God, might be nothing more than that of the permeating thoughts of those considered leaders of thought within the people, and as determined by the technology of the day and the communication skills that are available to those who would wish to lead. We can recognize too, that the voice of the people is never generally unified as one, but is divergent. In this divergence we have a majority and a minority, and as was experienced, the majority voice need not be necessarily right.

In this too when we listen to the voices of all the people, within the frame of a majority and a minority, these latter who are also God's people, that we hear the voice of God with the duality of its expression and as it is of nature.

In giving thoughts to governance we are brought to another concept of the duality of nature; that of spirituality and materialism which latter can be said to be expressed in its structure. We find here its structure determining our immediate daily thoughts and living, daily anxieties, hopes and fears, these daily experiences determining our aspirations for our future and the continuity that we seek in our human existence, all this now our humanity and the ground of our spirituality. With our knowledge and thinking we come to the realization of the circularity of the nature of governance in so far that the structure determines our system of thoughts and humanity and these them self determine how we structure our system of governance of the state, and of our businesses. The state provides us the parameters for our spirituality, whilst business our material needs. Within the circularity of the structure of the state determining our humanity and our humanity determining the structure of the state and governance there exists the ground for the construct and deconstruct of society as a civilized place, the enhancing or the diminishing of the quality of our lives; at the given point of either the structure of governance or the system of though of governance, or the pursuit of both at the same time. Where we have revolution in one and evolution in the other, this leads to some measure of instability, and move towards the breakdown in governance of the society.

In all of this we must contend with a phenomenon that arises in the extrapolation of thought within any perceived logic, that of the ideas coming to a situation of fallacy or incorrectness; or to a situation of not-knowingness. It is within these boundaries that we strive to govern through the creating of a structure for listening to the many and diverse voices of the people, giving thought to our humanity and its enhancement and our consequential existence.

Governance within diversity

We live in a universe of physical and material diversity in which we experience our not-knowingness, out of which our diverse spirituality of religion and culture is determined in providing us harmony first of all in the environment in which we find our self, and later to the wider universe. We each in our world appreciate its grandeur and its burden on us at times. Within this frame of grandeur and burden we coalesce, and at some point between these two poles we move to resolve issues in our lives and existence; emotionally and subjectively or rationally and objectively. We can seek to resolve these issues either within a frame of the survival of the fittest, or that of the survival of the fit. In doing so within the frame of survival of the fittest we move towards seeking to reduce diversity to that with which we are comfortable and which then parallels our humanity. In the frame of the survival of the fit, we seek to work with each other to enhance our situation through learning to appreciate the world of each other, seeing in it another grandeur of life and living as we naturally accept our own to be, all these being the expression of God. Where in our differences dysfunctions and deleterious consequences can be seen, we seek to resolve these not by the imposition of the will of one on the other, but by listening to each other and seeking solutions that enhances rather than diminishes.

It is in the situation of diversity and not-knowingness that we must search for our continued existence and wherein we seek help from each other, and even guidance, in the synthesizing and creating of the systems and rules and regulations that will govern our lives and our way forward. In this process of governance the leader, the governor, the people's representative then will not be a person who imposes one's will and wishes in the solutions of problems and the conflict that arises in the life and living of persons of diverse humanity, but one who will be able to hear each person and to help these diverse persons to articulate their perspective, as they are helped too to listen to each other and work towards a resolution and reconciliation of these conflicts and issues. The people's representative then becomes not so much the person who speaks on behalf of the people, but one who facilitates the hearing of diverse people and the resolution of problems that occur as each seek to live their life in diverse ways in society. It is in this that representative democracy is transformed in our western world and the Caribbean of today, to that of participatory democracy.

In Plato's democratic Greek city states it was sought to have people in governance who represented all that was best of the society, not from the slaves, but from the learned people in society, considered philosopher-kings then, and who came from their Guardian upper class and were trained in academia. The concept of he best of the people as governors has been accepted as the norm in all societies even when intrinsic to this is elitism, and which was so too in the Greek city states where the governing class came from this upper class of the Guardians, and was even considered above them when they went into the governance of the state. Elites can be open or closed and self generating one as was the case in Greece in respect to the Guardian class in general and the governing class, or an open and diverse one. In our societies today the governing elite is an open one, particularly in our democracies, where persons there are not only from one group or sector of society, but from varied classes and professions and sector such as business, academia, the church, the military, all working within what we identify as political parties. The commonality of these persons is that of the humanity that they share to serve in the governance of the nation, it being the highest level of service in the nation. Some do so for personal material well being, some for special groups and interests and we find amongst those a higher level of disconnect between themselves and society in general; while some others for the enhancement of the nation and amongst whom there is a greater connection between them self and society. A representative of the people today is more commonly drawn from a political party where this cadre of persons is considered to share a common perspective in major issues of governance then and its process.

Political parties of today, our new elite; is made up of diverse persons and of professions, and exists within the mantra of the survival of the fittest and is for the most part an open rather than a self generating one as occurs in other homogenous elite groups in society and this shows that representative democracy has value. However with a mantra of the survival of the fit, engendering a new spirituality and humanity, the structure of governance needs to be changed to accommodate this new system of thought. In representative democracy we select those that represent us as we are then, but in a new democracy we will select those who will help to make us who we wish to be in the future and this is best done within the frame and structure of a participatory democracy.

A participatory democracy will be one where those that are selected to govern will take responsibility for the creating of consensus between the diverse people through the understanding and appreciation of each other by systems and mechanisms that are created for this purpose. It will replace those that now exist which gave representatives the right to act on their behalf, and also the correcting of the misdemeanours of the governors in the governance process, and the people amongst them self struggling within the frame of the survival of the fittest for their existence. In this we find representative democracy generally re-active and negative, but in participatory the new frame in which structures and mechanism will be made, this will be given to being pro-active and positive. These structures and system of governance will be ones that allows for a continuing dialogue between persons from the diverse coalescence of the people, moving from their individual reference point in searching for a reconciling and synthesizing of these perspectives and not one of monologues by each with them using such tools as are available to them and in keeping with the might is right spirituality that flows from the mantra of the survival of the fittest.

The might is right spirituality is seen where yesterday's communication which was considered propaganda, has morphed; evolved; into marketing and or public relation activities of today, and where too underlying much of these activities there is intellectual dishonesty. In participatory democracy the structures and mechanisms for governance will allow for the diverse people and groups to have civilized dialogues in the putting forward of their perspectives in the search for solutions for the creating of the parameters within we all shall live our lives in harmony.

2.4. Governance Structure.
Democratic governance in the situation of diversity

The dominant structure of governance today in western societies of which the Caribbean is a part, is that of representative democracy where all adult people of a nation state select the person that they wish to represent them in the process of the governance of their state nation. The manner and system of selection of these representatives, governors, and the votes for these governors for doing so ranges from being that of a farce to that of being truly realistic in so far that a vote for a governor and the number of votes for the governor is true and reflects the intent and act of the voter at the place of voting. That which influences how one votes, usually the tools of communication, ranges from that which is consciously designed to be manipulative, to that of being genuine and rational consideration and concern about dominating issues of governance then. Within these nation states we have different forms of governance structures to reflect what has come to be accepted as democratic within the culture of this nation state and that which is enforceable by the state.

Considering the nature of human beings in that of the circularity of their streams of consciousness within the framework and spirituality of the superstructure of their governance and their everyday experiences, and this within the duality of nature, we recognize our ability to impact on the humanity of our being through the structure of governance and also the education of the people. We accept also that human beings are taught through their experiences and this has a far greater impact on their humanity than postulates. It is for this reason that societies that postulates the human equality of all but live within the mantra of the survival of the fittest and even where democracy is said to exist that there are however enemies inside and outside. The more farcical the democracy which is the situation where it is more postulated than practiced and experienced, the more enemies that the state will have, beginning with growing numbers within.

Caribbean and Jamaican diversity

Jamaica within the Caribbean is an island nation state where its people now all come from immigrants. Few if any of the original people of the land are here or have their blood flowing in the veins of the present people. We have Jews mostly originating from Spain, other European people originating from England, but also from Germany; Africans, Chinese, and East Indians. Accordingly we now as a people have within us the four main culture vectors of the world which are, first, the spirit of individualism which underlies the people from Europe and western societies, secondly, the spirit of collectivism that underlies the cultures from the east; thirdly, the spirit of rationality from the north from where we have the least, and lastly, and in the greatest numbers the spirit of emotionalism arising from the southern lands. We the people of the Jamaican nation and state are a blend of these diverse cultures. Through God's will, whichever God we acknowledge and however we worship him, we all have inherited a land that is for the most part more wonderful than that which our forefathers enjoyed. All our Gods would seem to have had the commonality of thought in considering us fit to be here at this place which many consider paradise. In this spirit it becomes our duty to all these Gods for us all to work together to make this place better for God and us human beings, ourselves.

In this our nation where we have people coming from families originating in diverse and different cultures it becomes easy to experience our everyday lives from differing perspectives and therefore in the state we would envisage people coalescing around several points of view and perspectives as a political party in the pursuit of the governance of our nation state The reality is that this is not so, and we give thanks for this to all the Gods we serve and worship, as our narrow political diversity of two main parties comes to the near duality of nature.

2.5. Participatory democratic governance structure
Parliament for participatory democratic governance

Jamaica has a democratic structure of governance that parallels the Westminster model, and also the western system of thought of the survival of the fittest, and too a political ambience where there has been for the most time of it being a nation state, only two dominant political parties. Whenever one of these two main parties at the event of an election finds itself with the larger number of representatives coming from its cadre of politicians, and by this being considered the winner, they take all the paramount offices in the governance of the nation state. It is within the spirituality of the survival of the fittest where might is right, this now in numbers, and where too, the winner takes all. In Parliament where all these representatives sit in pursuit of governance, the winners, the majority block, again in the process of taking all there is considered the Government, whilst the minority block, the losers are considered the Opposition. This creates in Parliament an atmosphere where the two blocks become involved in an adversarial struggle in the pursuance of the governance of the nation state, and Parliament, the place where many of the persons who seek to serve at the highest level in society, are demeaned and diminished, this also demeaning and diminishing Parliament itself.

The representatives from the minority party, called the opposition, persons like majority party and considered now the government, who seek to serve the nation and state because of being there in Parliament in a minority perspective frame find themselves in a role in which they must act negatively and consequentially destructively, rather than positively and consequentially constructively. In this role of opposition in the pursuit of the governance of the state they find themselves in a situation where to perform this task they must adopt a sophist behaviour and character. In the adopting of this behaviour and character in the opposing, and opposing and opposing this becomes over time embedded in them and then their humanity, and where their psychic energies are used more to deconstruct rather than construct.

When in the process of governance the situation for construct is recognized and deemed necessary these representatives within what then is called the majority, and called the government they then begin this process which would be more realistically considered reconstruct, as that which they then seek to construct, in many instances what they may well have helped to deconstruct. When this is then done from a unidimensional perspective it becomes dysfunctional early enough. Governance within these vectors of style diminishes rather than enhances a society and development in the quality of life for the citizens there. The construct of a civilized society does not inhere in such a situation.

Governance of the state would be better served by considering all representatives selected by the people as government, and where one would find a majority party block and a minority party block. This recognizes not only the representatives of the people who have a minority perspective, but also the people themselves whose voice is that of God and part of our diverse universe. In the governance of the state therefore we would seek to bring this minority perspective, one which is at times held by as many as forty five per cent of the people of the nation, into a positive and serious consideration of matters in the process of governance. A parliament or government where all the people's representatives are seen to be fit and worthy persons and respected, is one in which common ground can be sought and found in the process of governance and engenders first within all the people's representatives a sense of responsibility in their behaviour and character and this extends later to the parliament and then generally to citizens of the nation. It also invites more of the better persons in society to serve in the governance of the state. The nation becomes better poised to construct and spiral upwards as all the people's representatives are placed in a situation in which their psychic energies are being used in a positive and constructive manner in the governance of the nation state and which then becomes not the representative democratic governance of the state with high levels of dysfunctions, but one more of a participatory democratic governance with a lower level of dysfunctions. Within such a frame society is better placed on the path to becoming more spiritually and materially developed and ultimately civilized.

Ministerial policy making and participatory democratic governance

In the governance of the state we have areas of concern such as the matter of the health of the people, that of agriculture and that of education. Areas of concern are usually considered a ministry. Such concerns can be narrow or wide depending on how they are defined. In the situation of concern for health, education and agriculture there could be three ministries or two, where in the situation of two, the concern for health and education would fall within a ministry identified as human development. When it is recognized that our humanity and consequential character and behaviour rests within the frame of our material and physical self which gives rise to the concerns of our physical health, and then our mental and spiritual self which is for the most part impacted upon by education in the determining of our lifestyle that could be good or bad for our health, we find there a rationale for giving concern for both within such a ministry. In the concern for education it may well be seen that it is primary to our human development and that it is a greater determining factor in our human existence and development, and consequential capacity to contribute to society that it is dealt with apart from our physical well being. A ministry will therefore have what is to be considered one or more subject areas of concern, and the determining of this will rest upon the strategic importance of the subject area at the given time in the development of the society and in the affairs of governance then.

It has been the function of the majority party, and in particular its leader to select a person, usually one selected as a representative, from their party block to take responsibility for a ministry and area of concern. This person to whom this responsibility is given is called a minister, administering and managing this unit of affairs and concerns in the governance of the nation. The leader of the majority party block in parliament, who is usually also the leader of the party, is called the Prime Minister and the person who oversees the activities of these ministers through their office called the Prime Minister's Office. Collectively, the ministers, including the Prime Minister is called the Cabinet, the most powerful body in the governance of the state nation.

From the representatives of the minority party block a person from there becomes the leader of the Opposition, and who usually is also the leader of this party. This leader then selects from their block persons to monitor and give concern to the actions of the ministers in the pursuit of their ministerial activities in governance, and all these persons and the Opposition leader then called the shadow cabinet. Through these persons, the prime minister and the cabinet, the leader of the opposition and all the other representatives coming from what is called the lower house, we for the most part experience the governance of the nation as the representatives of the people interact in the pursuit of doing so.

A feature of this situation is that the leaders of these parties, the majority and the minority and interchangeable from time to time, must do all that they can, and this with continuity, in the constituency for which they seek to represent to assure their selection, and then to be in parliament as the leader of their block. This situation engenders actions that can be considered as manipulative at best and later lacking in integrity and of good behaviour and character. This structure of governance represents and expresses what is considered the people's will and within this circular frame of our humanity determining structure and structure then determining our humanity, and as is expressed in the governance of the state; and as it goes further too in the establishing the parameters for our daily lives. The behaviour and manner in which our representatives relate to each other, the respect and regard given to others in this process of our governance, impacts our humanity. This behaviour that reflects the spirituality and system of thought of the survival of the fittest and the winner taking all ;and the structure within which this is done; provides to the people in society the rules of engagement with each other in the living of their daily lives, and by so doing their humanity.

The affairs of a ministry are usually that of developing and recommending to parliament for endorsement policies for state organizations that falls within that ministry, and this is sometimes extended from policy concern to an operational one. Another activity of a ministry is the creating of laws and regulations which will determine the conduct of citizens and their behaviour in this dimension of their lives and living in society. The question arises as to how within what we consider to be a democratic state these policies and laws are developed. A minister of agriculture may well be selected to be such seeing that he is a person that is the representative of an area in which this industry is a dominant one. This could be said to be a good thing as this person has some knowledge in the industry, and particularly so of his constituents. This person as the minister who must deal with different dimensions of agriculture will be responsible for giving consideration to them in the form of policy proposals that will be presented to one's colleagues in the Cabinet and later to Parliament for ratification. The minister's thinking on the matter will be central to the policies presented and this will be based first of all on the empathy that one has for their constituents, this minister's own knowledge of the issues in the situation, all of this impacting on this person's continuing there in service as the people's representative.

In this we find education and rational reasoning on one hand and manipulative endeavours on the other. Another matter of concern here is the question as to whether or not what is good for the nation, and as is put forward by the minister, is so too for one's constituent. It is in issues and situation where there is a conflict of interests, this foregoing being just one of such, that we find and appreciate what is considered the collective responsibility of the cabinet, and decision making, and this generally from a political perspective, and more so than from a national and rational perspective.

One reflects again on the practice of the democratic governance in Plato's Greek city states where it was considered that the thing to do for the persons that were selected to be the representatives of the people in the governance of the state, for them to remove them self from their constituents and public at large and even their wives and families in order to be wholly objective in the process of governance and not to give favour to one or any above others. Out of this has come the concept know as platonic relationships and the other as that of dealing with matters at arm's length, in order to facilitate objectivity in decision making. Democracies of such times then were situate on the path towards being austere and autocratic, all on behalf and best for the state. In democracies of today it is generally felt that the people's representative should be close to them and share in their everyday existential experiences in order to effectively represent them. In these democracies we find them on the path towards corrupt, charismatic and subjective decision making in governance.

A decision making dilemma exist within both of these situations. Within the context of this latter situation, it can be considered that a minister of agriculture who represents a farming constituency is not necessarily the best person for taking decisions in which the national interest is paramount, rather than a geographic area and or product interest group. This might not have been just according to the sophists of Plato's era, as justice was said by them to be tri-partite; firstly, paying one's debt, the debtors then being the people of one's constituency. Secondly, helping friends and harming enemies, and thirdly, doing whatever was to the advantage to the strongman. This was the humanity and postulate of these learned men, and too as we understand it secure in their lives through their knowledge and learning. We understand too that in their society the general level of knowledge and learning of the people, that which we now call education was not as general and as high as it now is for the most part in our western societies This can be considered to be part of the progress and modernization there and in which we embrace the idea of globalization. Even however as we have today more societies where people are more widely educated, both in depth and of higher levels, and of other peoples of the world, than there was in earlier times, and where now too education is still less than training, paradoxically, there is to be found a larger number of persons not having certainty of things, either as being right or being wrong. Part of this is that of knowledge making one humble, and individuals going from this to not being willing or able to commit ones self to a moral perspective of that which is right or that which is wrong.

This human dilemma of our times arises partly from the fact that our society is more an informed and information one, and the consideration that information of which data is a part is education, which it is not. Educate, coming from the concept of educing implies knowledge from which parallel constructs can be had, and this through reasoning within some logic or frame and education then lies within this frame. In a singular parallel of information we induce things, whilst we use more than one parallel to educe for our conclusions in reasoning which is the essence of education. What is important in education is the honing of one's capacity to reason from the ground of knowledge and of parallel situations. When a minister of agriculture has knowledge and information concerning agriculture in general and in and of particular aspect of this he becomes more able to deal with the matter at a national level. When however it is at a narrow level, we recognize gaps there and the possibility that in inductive reasoning flaws and fallacies more easily arises in decision making, and this even more so the greater the extrapolation, and the further away in time.

The concerns of a ministry of agriculture may well impact upon the use of land and also the manufacturing industry and these subjects may well not fall within the ministry. The minister, whether educated, trained or informed in his subject will have therefore an immediate and wide gaps of not-knowingness and this situation will engender in the making of policies and law and order, ones that are highly flawed and faulty, in the pursuit of serving the nation in this concern. Where the Cabinet responsibility is more to the nation and the substance of decisions rather than towards the minister, the best of decisions inheres in that situation and the society in general is better served.

Aberrations arises in all our human endeavours, from time to time, some which are benign, some deleterious and some which are considered miracles because they are so beneficent. We seek at all times to reduce the deleterious and considered dysfunctional outcomes and results, and we do this by listening to others, perhaps with differing perspectives, some that may well be given more to the negatives than the positives of the situation and seeking to reduce the gaps of our not knowingness as we seek solutions for correcting such dysfunctions that are perceived. The listening to others by the minister is best done on a council set up within the ministry where persons of some diversity of perspectives arising from their field of endeavours, near enough to the area of concern of the ministry of agriculture, voices their thoughts and where together in this council they seek to make the best of synthesis of all that is said. Fallacies and flaws in policies and decision making are reduced and better ones that redounds to the nation are had in the situation. The minister serves best when he facilitates the business of the nation rather than only a constituency.

Ministerial councils and participatory democratic governance

A minister, a person responsible for the taking of decisions in the creating of policies on behalf of the people, in the pursuit of discharging this service within the structures of our present representative democratic state governance, does so in a situation of perceived dysfunctions. The first is that of the nearness in social space to certain interest to groups and consequent conflict of interest which can extend to corruption. The second is that of a personal and consequential unidimensional perspective either within the singular frame of experience that comes from training or of a wider one of education, which though is less likely to be deleterious, has however its limitations in so far that in all human beings each has their un-knowingness. The third vector is that of the disconnect from other ministry concerns that exist near enough to the concern of this first ministry and which impacts on and either enhances or diminishes the decisions taken there.

A mechanism for the removal and reduction of these perceived dysfunctions exists in the creating for a minister within a ministry, a ministerial advisory council. Such a council would be one that listens to the varying perspectives in respect to the ministry's subject and give concern to these in the developing of a synthesis on which policies are to be created. The council will listen not only to its members but it will also as a general rule listen to others who though are not a part of this council are interested parties in the matter, in the presence of the public or in private. The policies when developed in this manner are more likely to achieve the desired outcomes, or such that it will provide the greatest good for the greatest number. In the process of these councils listening to others outside of those with whom they empathize and who are perhaps in our world of today of another political party, we deepen our democracy, transforming it to a participatory one, and we begin to create new standards of behaviour for our survival. We move from the survival of the fittest to that of the fit and this is what will be experienced in the deliberations of the council and in the pursuit of serving in the governance of the state.

A ministerial council at its commencement will be a reactive mechanism of governance, but in due course it will become more that of a proactive and monitoring one. At the commencement of the work of the council there is likely to be many issues of concern that are seen clearly as being deleterious. In many instances as a consequence of the arising of a major and aberrant dysfunction it is desired to have a commission to enquire into the cause and the deeper than then easily seen effects of this dysfunctional aberration, and to make corrections to this situation. Where we have such commissions which are usually without any continuity, we obtain information on the situation but little or no correction of the situation, which is provided by a council that has continuity and is not only reactive but also proactive. The perennial and constant arrival and departure of commissions, evidences the need for the mechanism of councils that have continuity and which becomes in time, a proactive one that facilitates the spiraling upwards of decision making and effectiveness in the effectiveness in policy making and governance.

Ministerial Councils provide a continuity of concern as is desirable in human endeavour given the fact of our human inability to forecast wholly the future and the outcomes of our decisions. As we go forward in life and experience the future we find occurrences that were unpredictable impacting upon our situation, thus creating unintended outcomes and consequences, some benign, some deleterious, and some highly satisfying; miracles as we call them; but all these outcomes ultimately by the hand of God. One dimension of the unpredictable nature of the situation of governance is the changing nature of the people and relationships and their knowledge and analysis of their situation, which provides them the ground for acting in a manner that is personally beneficial. It is within this that we find corruption and unethical behaviour and the configuration and manipulation of situations for one's personal benefit, and which one calls too, exploitation. This is far greater within the system of thought of the survival of the fittest than that of the survival of the fit. The latter brings with it the ideas of responsibility, usefulness and graciousness, where serving others is paramount, rather than that of rights and forbearance where serving one's self is paramount.

Whichever logic or system of thought that guides there will always be need for adjustments and modifications, some immediate and others later, to most policies, and a council that has longevity is a mechanism most suited for this task. When the council would have impacted on the present system of thought and behaviour that underlies the concept of the survival of the fittest in the conduct of affairs of a ministry, firstly and modifying it to that of the survival of the fit, its activities could become less and would operate at a lower profile in society, even as it spirals gently and gradually upwards continuously, both in material and spiritual well being.

Ministerial council structure for participatory democratic governance

An advisory council for a ministry could be one in which the minister is a member or not, but reports to the minister. In a situation of participatory democracy, the people's representative whether from the ground of being a representative for one's constituency which allowed for the selection as a minister, or as the representative of the nation in general which is the task that inheres in the ministerial role, the minister would be a member of the council, even if not its chairperson. The first other members of this council after the minister would be persons recommended by the leader of the minority party block thereby giving respect to, validating and enfranchising in a constructive manner the view of people in society who voted for this minority party block. The survival of the fittest and the winner taking all approach value system thought in representative democratic governance is then transformed into one of participatory democratic governance and of civilized citizenship as the modus operandi of people in society.

Within society there are persons operating within an area of concern, perhaps narrower than that of the areas of concern of a ministry, some in an operational manner, and others in an intellectual manner who form into interest groups. The operational person in agriculture, the practitioner, is usually identified as a farmer, and will find one's self in an agriculture association in general, or a coffee farmers association in particular. Those of an intellectual disposition in agriculture, in general or in a specific area such as coffee farming, may well be found in the academic hall of a tertiary level institution of education concerning agriculture. The minister of agriculture would invite such common interest groups to recommend person of their kind to be a member and part of this council. Within the ministry of agriculture one envisages the most senior of the permanently employed state officers there would be a member of this council and whom may well from time to time delegate this duty to another officer from this state organization to act on this senior officer's behalf. One would expect further, that persons of expertise from a subject area of this ministry would be there from time to time to reflect to the council not only their expertise, but also development and operational concerns in the making of policies. Where the ministry has agencies, bureau etc. that falls within its purview, one would place on its ministerial advisory council, a person from each of these bodies to be a member there; perhaps the chairperson of the board for the body.

When the minister of agriculture comes to the position of being chairman of a council to give concern to agriculture for the nation at large, through being the representative of a constituency that is predominantly that of farmers, and perhaps that of a particular branch of farming and agriculture, the minister arrives there with the interests and concerns of these farmers. A possible conflict of interest may well arise in some manner between the interest of a particular branch of agriculture and that of the minister's constituents, and of the concern for these two groups being possibly diminished by a national concern. A resolution to the dilemma is the appointment by the minister of a person to sit on the council to speak to the concerns of the constituency, and importantly, to learn of the situation in which the minister must act not only to represent and serve the constituency, but also serving the nation and society. The appointment of this person is better done by seeking recommendations from the constituency, rather than making a personal choice.

The overriding principle for selection of persons to serve on the council is firstly that of obtaining as much as is possible, the perspectives of the many and dominant groups and interests that exists within the ministries and in the using of the perspectives in making decisions that will benefit both these interests and then the nation. In this there will not be unidimensional thinking and perspective in the process of decision making in the pursuit of governance. A second principle in the selection and appointment of council members is that this will generally be done at arm's length, rather than that of what could be considered as cronyism and populist pre-determination. In a council such as this where there should be no more that eleven to fifteen members and where members of political parties be no more than five persons, the dominant skill of the minister will be that of listening to the contending ideas, rather than to members, and the refereeing and synthesizing of these ideas in pursuit of the development policies and strategic direction for agriculture and the people of the nation. In a council of above fifteen members sub-groups interests more easily become the determining factor in policy making, rather than the logic arising out of the knowledge and subject manner and the nation's interest.

A ministerial council provides the central critical governance mechanism for a participatory democracy. It is where the best of the nation's minds meet in developing the policies under the guidance of the people's representative, within a framework of civilized citizenship. The policies and strategic direction so developed will determine the rules and regulations in which we of society will live, and which later will determine our humanity. The minister will take the council's recommendations to the cabinet, where its impact on other areas of concern and of other ministries may be considered and established. When all this is done, it goes to the lower house in parliament where the representatives of the people of the nation are for such considerations and refinements that is seen fit by these persons, and then to the upper house for any further and possible modifications by the persons that serve the nation in this house. In the lower house of parliament the representatives of the people having knowledge of the realities of life in which the people live give guidance and concern for the people and seek to serve their interests there as they serve the nation too. The upper house provides to these policies a scrutiny that comes from persons who have served the nation well, and accordingly gives further guidance on the road one should travel in making these policies more enhancing of the nation's situation.

Participatory democracy by the ministerial council mechanism is further enhanced when it listens not only to its members, but when from time to time it listens to civil society by a variety of approaches such as accepting and making recommendations in a process of stimulating and engaging them in this decision making process. One then in this exchange hears directly the voice of the people which is said by many to be the voice of God, the transcendental, inexplicable and imponderable spirit. It is now know that the voice of the people can be manipulated by their fellow human beings, even and also by those who put forward themselves as seeking to serve them, and this usually in the process of being selected as their representative. In a representative democracy, one in which the survival of the fittest legitimizes the winner taking all, the diverse and differing voices of the people and of God and as is reflected in many small groups of likeminded persons, find no place there, and in this way, and they then become alienated from the over riding mores and values of the nation. In a participatory democracy and within the structure of a ministerial council, more even if not all of the people's voice will be heard, and it takes us nearer to the situation when the people's voice as that of the nature of God that has provided us with universe of diversity is used in the governance of the state.

A ministerial council creates the basis for participatory democratic governance and reduces the tendency for dysfunction in the making of policies and programmes, and as occurs within the representative democratic governance system. The points from which dysfunctions arises there is that of the minister being close to one's constituents who expects of the minister, usually, to place their well being above that of the nation, and where when extended one finds corruption. The other likely situation of dysfunction is where the minister's education and or training become the major ground for a policy perspective and thinking. Within such a narrow frame of thought, more gaps are likely to exist and more flaws and fallacies to occur. The third situation of possible dysfunction that the ministerial council avoids is that of the disconnection of the concerns of that ministry with the concerns of other ministries in the state and which either impacts upon it or which it impacts upon, in such a manner that it reduces the effectiveness of this first ministry. Ministerial councils in this manner engenders better decision making in the pursuit of the governance of the state and nation.

Ministerial council and the lower house

In the process of governance the minister will bring to the lower house of parliament matters that the council has deliberated upon, for all the people's representatives in the state to consider. The minister can do so from two perspectives. The first can be that of the empathy and the feelings the minister has and wish to display for the people of the constituent whom he represents and the first reason for his presence there. Views of this constituent of persons might well be sought, and matters dealt with according to the feelings and perception of the reality of these persons. In this the minister seek foremost to represent the views of the people even if it differs from the general reality of the situation and in that regard it is flawed; and that also of the nation. The second approach is to advise and guide the constituents on issues and where it is flawed seek to correct this, and in parliament he represents this perspective. In the first approach there exists the possibility of a compromise of one's integrity, and as more a follower than a leader, whilst in the second it is lesser so and behaviour displayed is more so that of a leader.

The role of a representative in the governance of the nation as a minister has a duality, one being the dealing of situations from the reality of one's constituent and the other from that of the situation of the nation. The role here can be characterized as one of leadership more so, rather than that of a follower, where one is more likely to diminish one's integrity. As a minister coming to the lower house with matters dealt with by a council and one on which he was a part as the representative of a constituency, the most important character of the minister will be that of good judgment in their service to their constituency and further to the nation. This characteristic, when underpinned with the moral integrity of the survival of the fit, provides the basis for a truly civilized society.

Ministerial council and the upper house

The second house of parliament and part of our governance process is the upper house, one whose members are selected by the leaders of both the majority and minority party blocks. Matters are passed from the lower house there for review, assessment and evaluation, by persons whom it is considered have displayed high levels of competence and integrity in service to and within the nation. This house is considered the place for the review matters of governance objectively and at arm's length from a constituency and the perspective of an electorate, but more so from the perspective of what is best for the nation.

This house allows too for matters to be seen not only in the context of what is considered good by the people of the nation, but also in context of the realities of our globalized world. This second and upper house provides the ground for the highest level of service in the process of governance, where after the ministerial councils have considered a matter in the process of governance and the lower house has done so too, it comes to there for its consideration by persons of expertise experience and wisdom in service within the nation and for the nation and for some in the process of its governance. Where governance exists within a participatory frame rather than a representative frame and an upper house of such persons exists, it provides to the state and nation a place where the best of decisions and policies can be had and where the spirituality of responsibility and usefulness in the governance of the nation is the humanity of these persons.

The upper house becomes situate on the path to its diminishing and marginalization where it is used as a place for the development of persons to become representatives of a constituency within the nation, and where too the members are selected wholly from a political perspective, that of the majority or the minority party block, and within which some will later seek to represent the people. It reflects a corruption of the role and function of this mechanism for the obtaining of the best of policies and decisions which as the upper house it is created to provide and within which the highest level of service in the governance of the nation should occur. In the pursuit of usefulness in the process of governance of the state, and in the discharge of one's responsibility in society, and where this is done within a participatory democratic structure, the state and nation becomes better for this.

2.6. Monitoring of state effectiveness in a participatory democracy.
Monitoring of state organizations

Each public sector and state organization falls within a ministry, some directly and called the civil service, and others as operational units providing a service or goods to the society, within organizations that are identified as statutory bodies, these having a governance Board, or agencies. those without a board. The civil service has its monitoring mechanism, but the statutory bodies and agencies are without such with any continuity as they perform their tasks, on either a long term basis or short term. It is considered here that these state organizations in the performance the tasks they were set up to perform for and on behalf the people of the nation, should be monitored on a continuing basis and not only periodically such as annually, and this within a governance structure that facilitates a collaborative and collective behaviour in the pursuit of serving the nation and state. It is considered here that both these organizations should have a board, supervising and monitoring the activities of them, on the principle of participatory democracy and as is applied in the creating of a ministerial council. This would allow not only for more effective monitoring, but for being more proactive, and having a better decision making capacity.

As regards the organizations identified as agencies which usually provide a regulatory specialized service and which forms a part of the operational governance of the nation, the board could be more considered a supervisory one for dealing with the platform of its services as it also advises on the efficacy of its services.

Beyond the principle of the selection of the members of the board in a participatory manner, one would select members of the wider civil society interests groups that have specialized knowledge of the subject matter of concern, or of the operation platform of the agency. The latter type of appointment would apply to even statutory bodies. The chairpersons of boards would be appointed by the prime minister on the recommendation of the minister under whose portfolio the body falls. The chairperson of each of these boards would be responsible to provide to the prime minister's office regular reports, quarterly or more desirable every two months, on the operations and affairs of the organization. A copy of this report would also be sent to the ministry within this organization falls. This report will be developed from the reports from the chief executive officer which outlines the conduct of the affairs of the organization over the past month or the period for which the organization is mandated to report upon.

The prime minister's office on receipt of the board's report, would then submit this to a bureau of public sector performance which will then analyze and evaluate it and then advise the prime minister and the responsible minister. The organization's board will be the first level of monitoring on a continuous basis of these two types of state organizations, and the bureau of public sector performance management the second, measuring the efficiency of the body. The first monitoring would be done within the frame of a participatory democracy which is congruent to the system of thought of persons who seek to be useful in service to the nation and in pursuit of responsibility, rather than in the frame of a representative democracy of the survival of the fittest and in pursuit of the obtaining of benefits through rights for special interests and groups. The second measuring, that of the efficiency in the operations of these state bodies, would be done at arm's length by this bureau of public sector performance management.

Bureau of public sector performance management

The second level mechanism for the monitoring of the performance and review of government policies, and within which public sector state bodies discharge their functions is the Bureau of public sector performance management. This body which would be part of the prime minister's office and would be staffed by professional business and organizational analysts from both the public and private sector who would analyze the reports submitted there and then advise the prime minister and the minister who has responsibility for that body, on the results of their analysis, and on the manner in which the policies are pursued and goals of the state organization is being achieved, and how resources are being employed.

Analysts would serve no longer than two consecutive three year terms. They would be seconded from the private and public sector to serve in this bureau. The chief analyst, the chief executive officer of the bureau would be appointed by the prime minister upon the recommendation of the governor general. The governor general may well act in an advisory role to the prime minister in the staffing of the bureau and its management. In the pursuit of the duties the bureau becomes a repository of information concerning the policies and rules of operation of a great number of state bodies established in the governance of the nation. Accordingly, the bureau will be able to provide to the public, in keeping with the rules that guides this, access to information concerning the governance of the state, and in particular these state bodies. In this regards, the bureau with its information centre will provide transparency in the process of governance to all citizens. They will then be informed on an ongoing basis of the results and outcomes of decisions taken in the process of governance of the nations and when they select their representatives, they can do so more objectively than subjectively.

A bureau of public sector performance management monitors governance on a continuing basis and more proactively than reactively. There are at present state mechanisms that are created to monitor governance and this is done more reactively than proactively. These could be paced within the bureau, abolishing some and rationalizing others. The representatives of the people and particularly those now considered the opposition but of the minority block, would have more time and opportunity to be themselves proactively engaged, and effectively so too, in the serving of their constituents. When state organizations are more effective and efficient it becomes more possible for the representatives efforts to be seen in the serving of their constituents, and their endeavours more meaningful.

Within this participatory democratic governance process we find a high level of competence in the making of decisions ultimately emanating from the upper house of parliament, and then in its implementation in state bodies. This enhances the quality of life of the citizens of the state, and give to those who in the pursuit of being responsible and useful in the serving of the people in its governance, a deep sense of being.

2.7. Governance, responsibility and citizenship
Participatory governance and responsibility

The structuring of the boards of statutory bodies and executive agencies as considered here, the establishing of ministerial councils and a bureau of public sector performance management in the process of the governance of the society, deepens participatory democracy and also creates the situation where the people's representatives and other persons in the wider society work together in the service not only for one's self, but for the nation.

In this situation where people of the wider society are continuously engaged with each other, and persons selected as representatives are given the ultimate authority within a collaborative and participatory structure to establish the rules and regulations within which they must live and work together, they come to realize that it is acts of responsibility that provides the ground for their development, progress and the enhancement of their spiritual and material well being, rather than the actions that asks for rights and the forbearance of others, individually or as groups. In working for the society as a whole it will be noted that in the diminishing of each other we diminish and reduce our own ground and accordingly our capacity for achieving our goals. It will be noted that the survival of the fittest does not generally create material and spiritual well being for all, even if this is within the context of the greatest good for the greatest number. The ground exist within that context for the pursuit of self interest above others and coalitions may well be formed for this, such as community gangs with their dons or war- lords that control rural or urban areas, or a self generating capitalist or political elite, where in each of these coalitions they serve themselves first and widen and increase what is considered goodness through patronage to others for the purpose of the securing of their own elite social space and well being.

The persons selected from time to time to be part of the governance process, not to facilitate the pursuit of rights by individuals, but to facilitate people to work together in a participatory manner and within the wider society may well create coalitions to do so. This will engender the enhancement and development of society and as will be reflected in the policies that are formulated and the goals established and achieved. In this we find that the behavior by the representative will be considered as being responsible by their constituents and allowed continuity in this role of serving.

Elitism when grounded in responsible behaviour becomes more a contribution to society, rather than the accumulating of special rewards together with the social space and power and the capacity to control things there, and which allows them to favour that which one wishes, and particularly so for one's own self. Elitism that is grounded in responsibility and from which usefulness arises, facilitates and engenders participatory democracy, rather than one which seeks to facilitate that of rights as is done by representative democracy, and which is legitimized within the spirituality of the survival of the fittest. This elitism of a participatory democracy which is an open one, rather than a closed and self generating one, becomes as is necessary the centralized force which impacts upon the circularity of structure determining humanity, and humanity determining structure. It will enable a societal change in direction within the frame of responsibility and a continuingly spiraling upwards and enhancement of our human condition as reflected in the quality of life in society, rather than that of downwards where in the diminishing of the quality of life we have an increasing fear of our fellow human beings in society and where in the struggle to be the fittest, the need for personal security becomes an important dimension in our daily life and living.

In a participatory democracy the structures and systems there will enable representatives from both the majority and minority party blocks, likeminded persons in their desire to serve society and the nation, to work together in collaborative and positive and proactive manner in the governance of the society. The persons of the minority block are not demeaned and diminished in the pursuit of a life to be responsible and useful to the people of society. Their perspective and point of view find a place in the mainstream of governance and they are not pushed aside as it is now and as is legitimized by the subliminally embedded value system of thought of the survival of the fittest, and one in which the winner takes all.

Accordingly too, it does not become necessary for the minority to seek to negate the majority, considered winners in all they do. The psychic energies of the minority will be used in a positive manner to build with the majority, rather than seeking to destroy them, those who then will be the identified facilitators and point of focus in the endeavours of all the representatives in the pursuit of governance. Within this structure and system the need for patronage to others by the majority, not now winners or representatives will cease and be replaced by that of their competency and skills for the facilitating of the people to work together in a collaborative manner. A culture of responsibility will come then to underlie all the endeavours of people in society; beginning then with the political elite; and which is the basis for the construct of a civilized society. Elitism and in particular the political elite, grounded in the facilitating of the pursuit of responsibility out of which the enhancement of society obtains will replace the elitism where patronage and rights are pursued and which demeans, diminishes and in time destruct society as a civilized place and makes it into a human jungle.

Transparency inheres in the structure and system of participatory governance and in these state organizations where their activities impact directly on the lives of citizens. Malfunctioning of these systems due to corruption and irregularities is quickly and easily seen when we have there the presence of the minority party, and particularly members of the wider society in the form of persons from academia and subject interest professionals. The tendency for this is greatly reduced as cynicism and hopelessness in respect of treatment by the state, these being a source of alienation in society. This structure of governance too when it is ideas that are in contention and not the people, provides for the taking of better quality decisions as they are done within wider contexts and perspectives, thereby providing a wider frame in dealing with problems and the deriving of solutions, that makes for better outcomes for the people in society. In the situation too of the continuing concern for outcomes, the possibility for damage from dysfunctions are seen early enough, and for this reason adjustments and corrections are made to them, thereby enhancing effectiveness and efficiency.

This structure and system of governance creates an environment of collaborative and collective relationships in the pursuit of service to the people and determines in each participant a behaviour of civility and civilized citizenship as also a dominant spirituality of responsibility. This dominating spirituality of responsibility and civilized citizenship is one from which integrity flows and it is deepened between persons when the outcomes of their endeavors are experienced together. It provides to individuals in society the model of behaviour that is spiritually and materially rewarding and the enhancement of their humanity and self worth. In the spiraling upward humanity of people in society within the circular frame of the spirituality of serving and being rewarded, served and be served there will be an acceptance in society of the morality of responsibility and the survival of the fit.

Participatory governance and its morality of responsibility

The acceptance of one's humanity and the fact of the diversity of such that exists is for the most part created by the physical world in which we find ourselves, our nation and our community, gives one a consequential duty to these societal forces which so impact upon us and makes us who we are. In this duty there arises a morality of responsibility to contribute to the survival, continuity and, later, the enhancement of these societal forces. In the pursuit of one's contributions, we recognize and appreciate first of all the concepts of enhancement and that of diminishing, and next that of aberrant outcomes. Some of these may well be benign, some deleterious and dysfunctional, some extremely valuable.

The duty of responsibility that we have allows us to recognize actions and outcomes that enhances and to pursue these, and that in the outcomes of deleterious dysfunctions, to seek to minimize these; in the situations of benign dysfunctions to maximize or optimize these as we are best able. The situation of aberrant but valuable occurrences; miracles which we acclaim; we accept this and go further to use it in the identifying of God, the transcendental, imponderable and inexplicable and in ourselves, our ultimate not-knowingness. In the duty of responsibility that we have for contributing to the societal forces, it allows us to recognize that it is in the pursuit of enhancement, that which is right, rather than that which is diminishing; that which is wrong; that we find opportunities for this. Actions and behaviour that supports enhancement then becomes our moral duty and obligation. It is in this behaviour of the morality of responsibility, which exists within the system of thought of the survival of the fit, which underlies actions and behaviour that diminish neither individuals nor the society of human being.

A system of governance which seeks to have a morality of responsibility, must be one with structures that allows for all the selected persons of the people; governors, representatives of diverse interests and perspectives within the nation; to be constructively engaged in the creating the synthesis of rules and regulations which provide for the continuity and survival, and not the least the enhancement and development of our world and community and ourselves. The law and order obtained there from will be consequentially grounded in the acceptance of this morality and duty there and where it is becomes accepted later by the people of society that it is responsibility first and foremost that will be the ground of behaviour and relationships to those nearest, later, extending this to the governance of the nation.

When governors, the people's representatives serve the nation, they will do so within this moral frame that will allow for the expression of the responsibility of the people in general rather than that the moral spirituality of individual rights, privileges and entitlement. In the spirituality of governance, where the governors to give concern first and foremost to the morality of responsibility, there may well be found there the acceptance of the Kantian Imperative as a point of departure in thinking and the creating of law and order for society, that that which one does, should be such that all others in society can do the same, and this without the diminishing and demeaning of society and others in general. It is more so in the pursuit of responsibility coming from the logic of the survival of the fit and a morality derived there from that a society is developed materially and spiritually, rather than within the frame of a morality that is grounded in the seeking of rights for individuals and special groups of others all within the frame and logic of the survival of the fittest.

2.8. The fundamental spirituality of participatory governance
The determining of the behaviour of the governor

The structure and system for a participatory governance process around the mechanisms of ministerial councils and its selection from diverse coalitions of interest within the society, the creation of boards for all state organizations and the selection of board members in the manner paralleling the selection of members for a ministerial council, and a bureau of public sector performance management all of these being more proactive than reactive, allows for a morality of responsibility and usefulness within a very wide circle of persons in civil society. It allows for the bringing in to the governance process persons of goodwill, integrity and learning, all the persons who have offered themselves to serve in governance and have been accepted to do so by the people, thereby enabling these persons to be part of our democracy and being useful to the society that has nurtured them. It enables these persons of society through their contributions and usefulness in governance to have enriched lives, spiritually and materially, and by so doing create the culture of society. In this way one of the fundamental vectors of governance is seen, that of the determining of the humanity of human beings in society, and as will be seen now in their spiritual and material well being.

The considered structure and system of governance transform the selected persons of a constituency from a representative working from within its constituents perspective where it is possible within this logic, usually a narrow and disconnected one which sometimes can be to a great extent deleterious not only to the constituents but to the society at large, to a participatory consensual and collaborative one, where a situation may be flawed in its too great an extrapolation, can nevertheless be considered within its functionality, thereby enhancing the situation for all. This structure and system of governance also transforms the governor from either a so called leader or a follower to that of a facilitator, and a more creative role. In this role we find this selected person of a constituency giving service, not by placing a constituency perspective for consideration above all others in the contending perspectives that arises out of the diversity of our human situation, but also enlightening and guiding and acting as a reference point in the determining and governing ; the governor; for one's constituents. The greater the capacity for the governor to be a reference point for a constituency, the more the governor will contribute to the state, and displays then a capacity for higher service as a minister.

The determining of the behaviour of the governed

The role of government in society is to determine the parameters within which we must live and for us in the western world where our humanity now is determined within the system of thought of the survival of the fittest and individualism, and where we now find representative democracy, these are the parameters also for our governance. As we strive to be the fittest, our government sets the rules and regulations of the game of life of what is the fittest and how we get there, and ultimately, who then is the fittest. The game of life and living therefore becomes highly selectively and extremely reductive.

Within the system of thought of the survival of the fit the rules of the game of life are set too, but they differ from those that are made to determine the fittest, and so allow for more not to be diminished but to feel positive about them self and survive in the game of life and living. These rules of the game of life are the written rules and regulations of the state that provides what we call law and order and out of which we experience the spirit of the state. Within the spirit of these laws our spirituality is determined and the consequential mores and values which underpin our relationships with our family and community and further afield, in our nation state and the world at large.

This spirituality is further deepened in these governed and human beings in society; its citizens; when the behaviour of the governors, the persons selected by the people to set these laws, regulations and rules behave in parliament in keeping with the spirituality of the pervasive system of thought that underpins the structure of its governance. Where the system of thought underpins governance through the representative democratic process which is that of the survival of the fittest, individualism and the pre-eminence of the rights of individuals, there confrontational uncivil and violent interpersonal relationships together with sophist and intellectually dishonest argumentation becomes the nature of the people and their humanity in civil society. The progressiveness of this leads to some measure of development within society, but with a contamination that it self destruct within a short space of time. In the situation where the spirituality is that of the survival of the fit the humanity of the people in society will be transformed to one where collaborative and civil behavior towards each other obtains, and in the discharge of responsibility for each other's well being in society, material and spiritual, the quality of life for all therein will be enhanced. We come then nearer to being a wholly civilized society.

The style of point of reference in governance

The manner in which we govern ourselves moving from the system of thought to structure or structure to system of thought and in either to style, determines at a given time, our humanity and who we are as a people and a nation. At this time our structure of governance which patterns the Westminster model which allows for a selected representative; governor; to serve in governance for a possibly long and extended period has been considered to be dysfunctional to society and it has been considered that the length of time such persons should give service to the governance of the people and nation should be restricted. In the representative democracy structure of governance one implication is that a selected representative becomes disabled in moving from being a representative to becoming a minister, and then perhaps as leader of their party, and later to becoming the prime minister. This person is then restricted in the use of developed capabilities which usually occurs over time in a direct manner in the serving of the nation. Such persons however may well find opportunities to serve in the upper house.

In the limiting of time of service in a particular position there develops some instability in the governance situation and the affairs of the state. When limitation does not restrict a leader in the position as the leader of the majority party block, exercising state power and it becomes so that this leader must transfer power to another in the party to be able to serve the state at arm's length, the service as leader of the state becomes then ostensibly less powerful than the leader of the party. It is in the position as the leader of the party that power exists to select and give by patronage to the members of the party, the opportunity to serve the state in ministerial positions in state governance, and for the most part in statutory bodies where policies and operational endeavours are pursued. Restrictions in serving as leader of the party whilst serving the state then would be more meaningful than the restrictions made in the limitation of time as the leader of the state.

In seeking to correct the dysfunctions of representative democracy in respect of the wielding and the exercising of power within the state and a party by one person through the limiting of time of service to the state and not in that of political positions, this moves towards the creating of instability in the directing and development of the nation state, and the wasting of its resources. Within the participatory democratic governance process where the structure allows for the formation of a constituency perspective, extending to one on behalf of the nation, above that of a representative perspective, this is more valuable in the limiting of service by a representative and governor and could easily obtain more from the side of the constituent, the voice of the people, through de-selection and replacement.

There exists as is said by Sir Francis Bacon a duality in all things and as is shown in nature, beginning with the abstract and material. We then have negatives and positives and good and bad. Implicit in the concept of good and bad, is that of right and wrong. The concept of a good and right postulate if logically extended far enough arrives at a point at which it is fallacious and flawed. The concept of bad and wrong can be extended too to a point where it becomes seemingly reasonable and rational. This is the ground on which sophists thrive as they seek to make that which is ostensibly bad and wrong, something good and right, usually not in the far away extension of the situation, but in its immediate extension. In this duality we find differing perspectives and point of references in the solving of problems.

There is a political postulate that it takes cash to care. It can be construed from this that it is only when a parent is providing a child with the material things for which cash is required to obtain, that the child can be considered cared for, and for which it is legitimate for the child to respond and not in the counseling alone of the child in what this parent consider to be the expression of care for one's child, proffering to them this counsel that they might well have acquired by the trials and tribulation of their lives. Where a family of low income must sustain a family, it must mean that the caring spiritual guidance of the child or children therein must be limited.

This postulate creates the ground for dysfunctional relationships between the child and its parents, and consequential outcomes. In a situation which is driven by "it takes cash to care", one does not visit the sick unless one takes a present to this person or makes a contribution to their medical expenses, notwithstanding the fact that the presence of friends and acquaintances can provide to this person some spiritual uplift and encouragement that could put the person on the path recovery. In the life of a child and in assisting to give care to others there may well be need for cash to help in this, but in the contention that care can only exist within a frame of materialism for which cash is required, we arrive at a fallacious and flawed perspective of life and living. This materialistic perspective becomes deleteriously quite early in its logical extension, and is first seen in near relationships, and subsequently then in governance of the nation, where materialistic outcomes are more dominant than spiritual and human development outcomes, and too as it the determines the dysfunctions of the nation.

Another postulate is that we put people first, and this could be considered a human and spiritual reference point. In putting people first, the question is how do we treat with them, and treat them. Treating with them must be done in some order, and the question arises as to the order in which this will be done. Perhaps in the extending of this humanistic spirituality, one treats with the poor and humble first. The situation where a person has been strong and shown what one calls a sense of character, has striven and made a measure of success of one's life but is served last, this then gives rise to little or no spiritual desire or incentive; moral duty; to be so or to do so. We find here a paradox within the system of thought of the survival of the fittest, that the fittest ones to be served and accordingly treated first, are those who in seeking to be the fittest have at least become strong. To be strong, striving and of good character, and to be of service to others than to be not so, will then be seen as no more rewarding than to be not so. One finds in this reference point flaws and fallacies too, and when therefore we begin to have an increasing proportion of people in society considering them self poor and humble, we appreciate the impact of this postulate.

Moving from either of these two points of reference which then provides one with a perspective, one a materialistic and the other a humanistic spirituality, one can come to a situation of dysfunction, and where we have representative governance within a system of thought of the survival of the fittest and the perspective of the winner is that which guides the determining of polices, this obtains in due course. In the situation of participatory democracy, where the survival of the fit exists, the winner provides by the fact of being so, only the reference point in the beginning of the discourse for the determining of policies or rules or regulations or laws. In the discourse then and the recognition of dysfunctions that are possible in either situation, consideration can be given to these, and by so doing, enhance the quality of the outcomes, and to the benefit of the society.

In the melding of these two perspectives we come to a better resolution to the care and concern of people in society, and the manner in which one will treat with them. The level of the quality of melding will be a function of the quality of the referee and governor in the participatory democratic process which is pursued within the system of thought of a sense of responsibility, not only for one's self, but also being useful in society, and where too, it is appreciated that we serve ourselves best when we serve society well.

Chapter 3
GRACIOUSNESS

3.1. The ground of graciousness

Graciousness emerges first of all from the awe we experience in the grandeur, diversity and complexity we see around us and our not-knowingness in whole or in part of these things, some which impact upon us for good or bad, as they guide and direct all things in our world, thus making us humble. It is through graciousness that we diverse human beings with a commonality of a humanity of not-knowingness seek the path for continuity and enhancement of our lives even as we experience our diverse grounds of environment, grandeur and complexity from which our individual humanity, fears hopes and joys are first determined.

Graciousness goes beyond charity, which is said to be blind and in which manner many such acts are pursued in seeking to correct the deleterious dysfunctions of life within the parameters of the survival of the fittest. Within that system of thought and way of life graciousness is offered through the providing to all forbearance and tolerance by all, through rights, and where it becomes legitimate for the social space of one to be diminished and impoverished by another. Within the system of thought of the survival of the fit, graciousness there is a sense of brotherhood and the inclusion in the family of human beings in which there is the feeling of being bound together in the pursuit of our existence, each within a diversity that is separate from others, all of this within our sense of not-knowingness.

The spirit of graciousness arises further in us when we recognize God, the transcendental, imponderable and inexplicable spirit, has with an invisible hand created us in diverse ways. In the acceptance of the grace of God, we in turn must be gracious to him, by showing graciousness to his creation. Graciousness arising first in humility within us leads to nobility, this being a sense of care and concern for others much more so than for our own self. Accordingly nobility is not that which is granted but is recognized as existing within us and expressed in our daily living, and acclaimed and proclaimed by our fellow human beings in society.

3.2. Graciousness and responsibility

In the pursuit of life within the system of thought of the survival of the fittest, there is perceived the immediate occurrences of its deleterious dysfunctions, and to correct them in the spirit of charity rather than graciousness, rights are sought and when given are pursued within that spirituality, and within society. We find that in the pursuit of our existence within the beneficence of the granting of rights and within the rules and regulations and laws established, a deepened sense of being special obtains, which reinforces the humanity of apartness and individualism. The greater the beneficence that is sought and received the more one moves towards the encroachment and reducing of the spiritual and physical life space of others, and by so doing diminish rather than enhance and develop the whole in the discharge of responsibility to society.

We begin our human existence in a world with rights, first as the unborn child within the law and order of such, rather than a parental and law and order convention for the care of children. Then later in life we come to the rights to bear arms, carry guns. This latter right which many insist upon, allow us to appreciate the nature of society where this is seen as required to provide one with the sense of security and absence of fear of one's fellow human being, in the pursuit of one's life in society. In providing rights to the unborn life this is firstly exercised against the born life of its mother, from whom this unborn life flows, and then the state. These rights too in the form of entitlement, forbearance and tolerance, ultimately obtains from the other fellow human beings of society where these others have had no responsibility in the determining of its existence, but must then have such for it, and its continuity and existence in society. A paradox in the situation here is that of how this unborn life and child enforces their rights against the born and society; the nation state. In this too the child is being trained in the manner that it will live its life, now as a child and later as an adult, receiving without giving.

In all of this however one appreciates the desire to help the weak when one is strong and some sense of graciousness, and the unborn first and the child second could be considered weak, where the elder born ones; and particularly their parents ; are strong. The efforts to be gracious to reduce dysfunctions that arises because such actions are pursued within the frame of rights, creates further dysfunction and deepens the situation of the diminishing of people. The moral act and one of good intent, that of the helping of the weak, which is afforded to one living within the system of thought of the survival of the fittest becomes flawed because it is pursued within the context of rights and the dominant spirituality there from of individualism.

Machiavelli (1469 -1527) in his writing of which "The Prince "is the most renowned argued essentially that the means, such as knowing how not to be good, dispensing violence, not eschewing of deceit; all or any such actions, considered bad, find their justification in the pursuit of the political end of making the state a stable one. This value system which was formerly for state governance has become now the spirituality of the people and used in general, and considered as the means, and of any type, justify the ends. It is now one within which a large number of people in western societies live their lives such that it could be considered an acceptable norm of behaviour. In this we have evidence of how the spirituality of the governors determines the spirituality of the governed.

Martin Luther King Jr., (1929 - 1968) argued that the means are not separate and disparate from the ends, but are a continuum of actions and reactions like a flowing stream, and so if the means are flawed and corrupt, the end will also be flawed and corrupt. We recognize that this certainly will occur in the near end more so than in the far end. The far end however allows us reflection and opportunities for the correction and reducing of these flaws and indeed it is in this frame that the sophists seek to make that which is wrong into being right. In seeking to reduce and correct the dysfunctions that exist within the system of thought of the survival of the fittest, through being gracious and grounding this in rights, the results becomes a flawed, dysfunctional and corrupted one. That is why in his struggle for the equality of civil rights for the black people in USA, he adopted the style of Mahatma Gandhi's passive and peaceful protests against the British in India in doing so, rather than acts of violence within the spirituality and frame of the survival of the fittest.

In the situation of the survival of the fit, the mother in exercising responsibility for her child, unborn or born would discharge this concern within the convention, rules, regulations and the law and order of a family life act. This would define the role and relationships of the mother and father and the state in a supportive role within the context of responsibility. In such codes of behaviour where the spirituality of responsibility is more dominant than rights, and the state sharing in this responsibility, we find a collective responsibility, and of graciousness. Within such law and order which would be of more of a proactive nature and one which engenders responsibility rather than that of a reactive one that affords rights there would be dimensions of support by the state to correct and reduce dysfunctions that it is considered could arise in family situations, as it shows graciousness in assisting the mother and father to be. A family life code of convention of rules regulations and laws within the morality and spirituality of responsibility, for the care and concern for our fellow human beings, particularly those most vulnerable, and which seeks to enable the child to be considered fit to survive, and one too that seeks to correct deleterious events that occurs from time to time and as is nature, expresses graciousness in the pursuit of life and living. Individual responsibility sets the ground for and enables collective responsibility of the state and is extended further as graciousness where individual responsibility fails.

Where we give graciousness individually or collectively as the state and we receive graciousness as a consequence we find ourselves being responsible and civilized and this extends not only to the family, the near community and the state nation, but to the world at large. In the seeking for and the receiving of rights which begins and ends in our selves, this creates a sense of entitlement and divisiveness and disconnect from others in society. Kindliness flows from one's self to all other human beings in society, and so we create and construct civilized and cohesive communities.

3.3. Graciousness and religion

As we live our lives and experience occurrences which impacts upon it, and with the realization of our ultimate not-knowingness of much that we find in our diverse environment, we accept the existence of a transcendental spirit and force outside of ourselves that is to us imponderable and inexplicable. This spirit and force we identify as God, and from which flows a religion. With the acknowledgement of God we pursue our life and experience occurrences that regularly and with certainty impact on it and other occurrences that do so irregularly and with uncertainty, all of these determining our existence. Out of this we then create science on one hand, that which then are able to predict and on the other hand our religion that which we are unable to predict but both giving us the harmony within which we must live our life in this diverse universe. The rising of the sun and its setting in a desert of sand and heat, allows us to experience our God there and create our religion within this experience differently from its rising and setting in the forests of cold snow, where in the acknowledgement of a transcendental spirit we experience this differently and express this differently in our religion. Hence we experience God in this universe in diverse ways and express this in diverse religions.

In the pursuit of our humanity within the frame of our diverse religion we from time to time use violence against each other as legitimized within the survival of the fittest. We do this in words and deeds and seek to destroy others in the name of God ;Our God, the true God; within the frame of our religion which gives us rights over all others, rather than a responsibility for all human beings, that of the creation of that transcendental, imponderable and inexplicable spirit, God. The implied argument here is that God's work is unfinished as is seen in the diversity that now exists, and each of these religious groups is now left with that unfinished task to make us all into one, perhaps by selection as to whom is the fittest, rather than the acceptance of this diversity and acknowledging the wisdom of God in the creating and allowing of this diversity.

It is said in one religion that if one's hand is causing offence, that limb should be cut off. In juxtaposition in another religion which deeply determines the governance and laws of the state where this one exists, it has been the norm that when one steals, causes an offence to one's fellow human beings, that one's hand is cut off. We see in this that there are some things in all human societies that are considered to be wrong, and which causes an offence to one's fellow human beings, but the correction of which is dealt with in different frames of thought, and morality, that of religious mores. In the former religious order, it is generally considered barbaric to cut off the hand of a person who steals even if the religion accepts this act as wrong and an offence to others, and so we find contradictions as we find differences in treating with that which is wrong..

Religion is that which generally allows us to accept our individual not-knowingness and limitations and provides us with a frame for our existence with harmony between the people with whom we co-exist and the diverse environment within which we come into this world. When we observe the fact of the diverse religion each of which arises from the commonality of the notion of God, that which transcends us, we are left however with a choice within two frames. The first is the pursuit of our existence within this diversity and seeking to reduce it, perhaps even destroying it by violence, to that of one's own and within the context of the survival of the fittest and which one considers then the best for one's self, and all others. The other choice is that of co-existing and collaborating on common grounds that we find in this diversity, and searching for others within the context of the survival of the fit. We see already that common grounds exist between some of these one of which is exemplified in that of seeking to ascertain in society that individuals do not act in a manner to diminish each other through unsavoury acts such as stealing.

Religion can be said to be the broadest ground in which our character is conceived and moulded thereby determining our humanity and providing us the frame of thought that allows us to accept and treat with the daily transactions and impacts in our lives, particularly those that begin from outside of ourselves and our immediate knowledge. It becomes a paradox and human dilemma when we with our not-knowingness inject into religion some knowingness that we ourselves do not have and can hardly perceive and then see this as the ground for living our lives in separation from others. Religion which arises out of our fundamental humanity of our ultimate not-knowingness is the first basis for the formation of our humanity and when we come to this understanding we also become able to learn to live with all peoples of the earth, acknowledging and accepting our diversity.

When we treat with religion within the context of our not-knowingness and the survival of the fit, we create the ground and opportunity for the engendering of a wider range of human experiences and choice in our existence. By doing so our humanity is enhanced and graciousness engendered in our daily life and living.

3.4. Graciousness and civil society

In every society there is some commonality of behaviour of the people there that identifies and defines them, such as that which makes the people of Italy Italians, the people from USA Americans, and there are books written about these behaviours. For us in the Caribbean, the commonality that identifies us is our warmth as a people and the easy embracement of others being part of this. Most of all however, is that of our recent history of slavery. Within many nations and of their history, near and far, there has been slavery and other features of subservient bondage of one group of people there to another, as it has been in the Caribbean, all of this being considered then to be within the morality of whom is fittest. This morality of whom or what is fittest is another vector of the commonality and of our humanity and which transcends our being Italian, or American or Chinese or Indian. This is quite deep in western societies, where it exists there within the highly articulated system of thought of the survival of the fittest, and which is said to be validated by natural selection that is seen in the physical adaptation of animal and plant life to their environment and consequential survival there.

It is to be observed that there exists differing natural environments and boundaries which provides us first with the situation of a diverse world, and that which survives well within a certain environment fails to do so in others, while doing even better in others. It is observed too that within all of these environments there is usually diversity there and our reality is that the universe is more characterized by diversity than uniformity. The reality therefore is not the survival of the fittest, but that of the fit. In the derived spirituality of this misconception of the reality of physical and material universe there has developed a morality of the survival of the fittest and the mitigation of its deleterious dysfunction through the providing of rights for this, rather than the recognition of the survival of the fit. As there is no perfection in this world, and as this is more congruent to reality, a morality of such will be much less deleterious and dysfunctional and where this happens, this can be mitigated by graciousness. The transcending of the concept that survival occurs by being the fittest within the frame of what is considered the certainty of science and knowledge, over that of our uncertainty that arises in the situation of our ultimate not-knowingness, and the experience of our immediate physical and material universe, as the major determining factor in the spirituality of our life has been made so that it is the physical that determines the fittest, with slavery in the near past being one expression of this.

In the survival of the fittest and with the material and the physical being the determining of this within society, might becomes right and as it legitimizes the winner taking all. It is within this system of thought of the survival of the fittest that the commonality of behaviour from which individualism is nurtured that the ground for the morality of western societies obtains. Our democracies reflect a benign expression of this fact of might is right and as is reflected in numbers, and that which determines who should govern a nation state. The structure of governance then reflects this spirituality to allow for the winner taking all of the power that exists within the nation state and the winner then is enabled to determine most of what will be in society and which later impacts and determine our experiences there, and then our humanity. We have now learned that might in numbers is not necessarily right, and too, that the voice of the majority of the people is not necessarily that of God and as we hear too the different voices of God in the diverse religions, all of this within our not-knowingness.

In our lives and the daily interactions for our existence we recognize the occurrence of phenomena, many that are usual and for which we can predict, and others that are unusual and which we cannot predict. These latter we consider as aberrant occurrences, and which can be benign or dysfunctional, and it is in these that we first experience our not-knowingness in this universe of diversity.

In all of this we live our lives determining what is good and bad, right and wrong and shaping our morality and the determining of our actions of graciousness in the furtherance and enhancement of a civil and civilized society.

3.5. Graciousness and the state

Participatory governance has been part of our human history where this existed in clans and tribes in Africa and elsewhere, and where in the governance of a community, the Chief as it was in Africa, sat with members of one's tribe, or clan to take decisions in the pursuit of their life and living. This was a part of life and living in parts of Africa, in the latter decades of the last century. As communities, societies, and nation states grew, all the people therein could not sit together at a table to participate in discussions in the process of decision making or even go to war with the Chief as the leader in battle. One selected persons to do so, the army, on the behalf of the people of the community, as too one selected representatives to govern then, the first of these been considered Elders. In Africa representative governance was parallel to participatory governance as the Elders with whom the Chiefs ruled, were persons who lived close to and walked and worked with the people of the tribe, the village and the community. In Europe this was less so as the Kings and the Dukes and the Lords of the governing class did not occupy the same societal space as occurred on the continent of Africa in general. In the democracies of today for the most part, one participates only in the selection of a governor as one's representative, and this is for many only that which we are able to do in the expressing of ourselves and any perspective that we hold in the governance of our nation.

A dilemma today lies in the fact that in society people generally have a higher level of understanding and appreciation of our near and far world, but due to the greater numbers in societies, it has become so that where earlier an individual was one in ten they are now about one in perhaps a hundred. This factor reduces our individual value in a material and physical manner as we become less able to participate in the governance in society, but in which we are now more able to participate in a spiritual manner. We have on one hand more persons being able to make a contribution to the governance of society through the incorporation of their knowledge in the making of policies in the governance process of the society, where on the other hand it has become larger and more diverse, requiring more complex responses in the governance process. However, rather than creating structures in which a greater number of persons with learning can participate and serve, be useful and responsible; representative democracy responds through the providing of individual rights to the people, and many of these within a frame of sectional interests.

In our diverse and complex society, few if any of the representatives have the broad knowledge and understanding of the multiple and complexity of issues that confront the people there, for them to make meaningful contributions on each issue that requires the determining of the policies, rules and regulations for the society nation state, in the near community, from which they come as representatives, and later to the far one, the state. In our societies of today each of us in general, have our own special area of interest and the interconnectedness of each individual to the other in each of these areas of interest, and to society is not generally made. In the pursuit of depth of analysis within narrow frames, which brings one to the narrow dimensional perspective of science, which has served human beings well enough in some societies in the material aspects of their living, there has been a foregoing of breadth and interconnectedness of issues.

It is in governance and the pursuit of life and living in society where it becomes possible for this connection, and through the people's representative in the role of as reference point for the meeting of the minds of the people, in the issues that impacts on the existence of individuals in society. Governance is better done by listening and the era of today lends itself to this also, to our fellow human beings in society concerning their fears and hopes and having them participating in the voicing of these as it is sought to determine the parameters of their existence. In the creating of these parameters this rests not within the representatives themselves, but within the people in general, and the creating of structures and opportunities that enables the people to meet and determine their situation with their representative as referee and reference point. This becomes participatory democratic governance where authority and power come not from one's position as a representative and governor, but from the skills that enable the wisdom of the people to be expressed and for them to appreciate their interconnectedness and that their problem solving within this frame has greater effectiveness. This participatory governance, the essence of which is people power, is enabled by their representative and where people interact and become gracious to each other, thereby creating and enhancing both their material and spiritual well being.

Where the state in the process of governance creates the opportunity to meet together and participate in the resolving of problems in an objective frame, and where interconnections are made through the guidance of the people's representative, we engender graciousness of each individual to the other in society. This objective frame within which graciousness can be engendered was sought by Plato's republic, a smaller and less complex society in comparison to today's societies, and was done by the representatives of the people, the considered philosopher-kings, being removed from the people in general and even their families, so that they could deal with matters of the state and of the people at arm's length and with the greatest of objectivity. It is within this objectivity of the resolution of issues that we find the ground for civilized relationships in society, and consequential graciousness of each person to another.

In the acceptance that our humanity is derived from human society, near and far, we will appreciate that we have a responsibility to our society and to our fellow human beings therein, and that this comes before the claims of rights and forbearance. When in the governance of the society the structures for this is so done to reflect the acceptance and appreciation of our humanity and responsibility, and where within this structure and frame we use our talents in an objective pursuit of governance for the people in general, we create with continuity a gracious and civilized community.

3.6. Graciousness and law and order

Societies exist and their continuity obtains where there is law and order flowing from a morality out of a system of thought that determines what is right and what is wrong and what is good and what is bad. If there was no right to be considered good, there could be no wrong to be considered bad. In the reality of human pleasure and displeasure of the senses one would pursue whatever action pleases one, even to the matter of wittingly and willingly placing one's hand near or into a fire. Such an action causes pain to any human being. Even if for some this pain could be considered a pleasure, it is considered by most others to be a perverted one, but more importantly, one that could so damage a person that one becomes permanently handicapped and consequently of diminished capability to survive, and later becoming a burden to others. One is taught when one is young and unaware of the consequences of such an act; the hurting and diminishing of one's capabilities and the burdening of others such as the family ; that the putting of one's hand in or near to a fire; that it is wrong to do so.

Actions of children which are mostly of innocence; that of a greater not-knowingness than that of adults; are the ones more generally likely to do wrong things to themselves and to others are the concern of their family and the near community and from which was developed in Africa that the child was not only the responsibility of their parents, but also of the near community, the village and from where we have concept that it takes a village to raise a child. It is out of this shared responsibility, called collective responsibility, that we establish rules and regulations, law and order, that determines our societies as it creates our culture and humanity. With people from Africa being the larger number of people from which we of the now Caribbean people are descended, this underlying culture of humanity of responsibility existed here in our villages and districts amongst the people, for the care and concern for the children there and this later, given our small island physical space, created a culture of warm relationships which was extended to others in our social space.

In the pursuit of an activity whether or not it pleases one, the possibility exists that one can diminish not only one's self, but others, and society ultimately, and the necessity arises for society to protect itself from such behaviour. This is done by the accepting of responsibility for each other as we serve ourselves, determining what assists our continuity and enrichment, and so avoiding its diminishing. Actions that allows for the construct and continuity of society as it enhances too our lives and that of generations to come, are considered right, and those that deconstruct through the diminishing of our lives and the continuity of society are considered wrong. The concept of law and order is grounded foremost in the pursuit of what is right and it exists within a frame for the collective well being for all of the individuals in society. Actions for the satisfying of one's pleasure above that of others and which is the humanity of individualism, pursued then within the frame of what is considered one's rights, easily becomes destructive to the collective well being of people. It is within the frame of responsibility that one becomes assured of construct.

Within law and order and the pursuit of doing what is right we recognize aberrant occurrences flowing from our endeavours from time to time, some of which are at its best deleterious, and some at its worst benign to our human existence, as far as we are able to perceive them. In the construct of our law and order we do this so that we can construe graciousness there, thereby enhancing that humanity and spirituality in society. Aberrations occur outside of our control and usually in pursuit of actions which is meant to contribute towards the achievement of the goal of the increase of well being of society and its continuity, and accordingly the displaying of actions of responsibility. Forbearance or rights then given in such aberrations is more that of graciousness and expression of support for the individual in the pursuit of responsibility. This graciousness flows from society's collective moral might of responsibility.

When rights are pursued with a disconnection from responsibility and usefulness, graciousness is reduced and coarsened whilst vulgarity and violence are increased. Law and order will be pursued consequentially within the frame of might is right, leading to further deconstruct of civility. Law and order, pursued within a frame of responsibility and usefulness which then determines right and wrong, constructs and allows for graciousness and a society of civilized people.

3.7. The moral measure of graciousness.

Some things are right and some things are wrong and law and order in every society is based on this concept, and of what is right and what is wrong. Stealing and child abuse is considered wrong in most societies, if not all, and such matters are given concern in the law and order of the state. In earlier Jamaica most of the people were black and poor and it was considered wrong for such persons to vote in like manner that it was wrong for the slaves in Plato's democratic city states in Greece to vote. For black people in the Southern USA states, it was once wrong to ride in the front seat of a public transport bus. In UK it was once wrong for women to vote. What was once wrong has now become right through the expression of the spirituality of a morality of responsibility. The spiritual might of the morality of responsibility, engendered an accompanying physical and material might, such that it has made actions that were once considered wrong but had this nature of laying the ground for that of enabling a person to optimize their humanity and talent in being useful in society and contributing thereto, and which was denied its expression through the law and order there, to that which is now right, and into individual rights, and a civil right.

Stealing and the abuse of children are void of a morality of responsibility and have no ground from which usefulness in society can arise and which would engender a spiritual might such that it could transform this behaviour into it being considered right, and from which rights and or civil rights of those who pursue such acts, be placed above others in society. The abuse of children distorts their humanity; spiritually now, and even physically; diminishing then as adults later, and society. Stealing, the appropriating of and depriving of others of that which belongs to them, creates a sense of insecurity and fear of individuals in society and accordingly diminishes the quality of their life. An implication in the situation of stealing, particularly the things that one has acquired as reward for service to others, is that this diminishes in the individual the will to continue to be of service, thereby affecting the immediate and general well being of society. In the giving of rights to women to vote, black people to vote and to ride in buses in whatever seat available, all this now considered the granting of human and civil rights, one creates a situation where the lives of these people are enriched through the acknowledging of their individual value. This then allows them to have self worth and consequently to be more useful to society through releasing fully and freely the expression of their humanity and talents to the ultimate benefit of all in society.

Law and order that flows from a morality that is within the system of thought of responsibility and which allows for the engendering of usefulness and enrichment of human beings in society, has a spiritual might of right out of which rights flow. It is a law and order where the human physical and material self is connected to the mental and spiritual self and which defines us as human beings and above that of a law and order not so connected and is purely physical and material, and where it is that might is that which determines what is right. In the situation where law and order is mostly predicated on the material and physical dimension of our selves and which leads to a might is right morality, therein is engendered the coalescing of individuals around interests and concerns that are for the most part inimical ultimately to the general interest and well being of others and society. This coalescing into many groups of self interest creates a fragmentation and disconnect of one from another, leading then to the deconstructing of civil behaviour, which in time becomes reflected in high levels of violence. It can be seen here that at the individual level or in any group coalescing around a particular action and or behaviour which enhances the well being of others without the diminishing of others and society, and that when law and order is created within this frame it further strengthens society as it enhances the lives and the humanity of people there as the society spiral upwards in being a civilized one.

It is in actions and behaviour flowing from a morality of responsibility and where we find the enhancement of individuals and society that we find that which is right and it follows from this that actions and behaviour that diminish another or society is therefore wrong. Immanuel Kant (1724 -1804) who has as his major work "Critique of Pure Reason "gave us as an imperative rule of behaviour, that when we are about to pursue an action, when this is being considered, one should ask one's self the question, that if all persons in this world were to behave and or act in this manner, what would be the outcome for society and the world. Would it be enhanced or diminished. If enhanced, it would be the thing to do, that which is right and if diminished, not the thing to do, wrong. He also gave the imperative that one should not tell a lie. In the first of these two imperatives there is implicit there the equality of all human beings where one does not have rights, human rights, above that of others, and to concern one's self with one's own desires and benefits above the well being of others and society. Implicit in this we find the expression of a morality of responsibility, as also the concept of the equality of man.

When one has stolen, one would have pursued an act that diminished another and one which, should all other individual in society pursue this activity, this would diminish and deconstruct society as a civilized place. When in an act of charity with the quality of blindness that is found within societies characterized by the mantra of the survival of the fittest, one seeks to the ascertain the sustaining of the rights of this person who stole, without any concern for the person's morality of responsibility and too any concern for the person diminished in the situation, in this disconnect we not only diminish the morality of responsibility and usefulness in society, but move towards the deconstruct of a civilized society through reducing the value of law and order therein.

An act of responsibility by society out of which graciousness would come and which would strengthen both the individual and society would be one that enables the individual to use positively in some manner their talent, such as that which was used to diminish someone by stealing. It would do so first in using this talent or any other to correct the diminishing of the person from whom their property was stolen, and then go further to enable this person who stole to use this talent or others of theirs to contribute in the frame of being a citizen with a humanity of responsibility, to society and from which they obtain sustenance in society. The essence here is the morality of responsibility leading to serving and then being served. In considering this act of stealing within the frame of graciousness as an aberrant and dysfunctional occurrence, one would seek to make this bad situation a good one by placing the person who stole in a somewhat controlled one, in which they can be directed towards enhancing themselves through the use of their humanity to first correct the dysfunction that occurred and next in the development of their own self and human situation. When they find themselves out in the wider civil society their enhanced humanity and self arising through the honing of their skills and talents within the situation of the control of their life by the state, makes them less likely to live their lives in a manner that such dysfunctional occurrences arise and more able to contribute there to in a responsible manner. It is within a system of thought of responsibility, usefulness and graciousness and a morality there from that connectedness to one's fellow human beings and society arises most and when law and order rests within this it strengthens as it makes the society a more civilized one. Where aberrant occurrences that are dysfunctional are within the frame of graciousness minimized, it underpins the morality of responsibility, and the determining of what is right and what is wrong, enhancing the lives and the existence all in society and the quality of their lives. It civilizes individuals as it civilizes society.

In the proclamation and the acclamation of rights of individuals and the pursuit of this which begins and ends within individuals and above that of others in society and this so in endeavours that diminishes others and with the wish for the continued well being of such persons and such to be provided in the frame and logic of tolerance of the individuals, one moves towards the deconstruct of civility of one towards others and a civilized society and making it into a human jungle, rather than its construct. It is in the pursuit of responsibility, and usefulness and its mitigation of dysfunctions and the proclamation and acclamation of such endeavours within the frame of graciousness that constructs a civilized society where our human situation and humanity is enhanced and as will be reflected in the quality of life for all therein.

Chapter 4
CONTEMPORARY ISSUES

4.1. Issues of morality

In the life and living of individual human beings one becomes aware of two certain things. The first is that one never has the complete answer for all that one experience. Out of this measure of not-knowingness and not having the ultimate answer for things, comes the appreciation that there is some force or spirit above and beyond us all. This force and spirit is considered and identified as God. The second is that early in our lives we come to know and accept that the world has parts of it that are hot and parts that are cold, and that the needs of people in each of these parts differ. Our not-knowingness and our needs in these diverse places where we find ourselves provides us with a context in which we seek harmony with the spirit and force that transcends us ; God ; and around which a religion for the most part is shaped.

Another dimension of our human existence is that there are certain actions that we can depend upon for certain results and outcomes. Some of these outcomes, even if they do not occur one hundred per cent of the times wholly in the manner that we have come to expect it, one considers that it is better to act in this manner rather than another. Where the outcomes of acting in this manner provides what is generally wished and considered, then this is considered as doing what is right. Where the outcomes are not what one generally wishes or is expected, this is identified as wrong. It is out of this that we find the idea of that which is right and what is wrong. When the outcomes, results, of actions benefits not the individual in particular, but the community near and far, and which could be extended to the wider world, we consider this a moral behaviour and that which is right. Where it harms the near and far community and if extended further it would continue this harm, this action is considered immoral and wrong.

In our world of today which has become a global village and we in our daily lives relate with persons of varying religions and cultural background we need terms of references, the fewer the better, for our behaviour which will help us to make these relationships harmonious ones. Such terms of behaviour, morality, will be beyond one's individual religion and culture, though it is to be appreciated that there are common factors in many of these. There is none known to accept that thieving is right or the assuaging of one's sexual desires with the very young is so too.

Secularism and secularists exist outside the frame of a religion but within some frame of thought and values and attitudes, wittingly or unwittingly, which determines their behaviour and conduct and ultimately what is right and what is wrong. When tolerance of any and all human conduct and behaviour is considered right, and forbearance of this as human rights the question arises if there is such a thing as human wrongs; actions and outcomes. In this situation the conduct and behaviour now identified as intolerance becomes too, human rights and behaviour that must be tolerated. The action of one who when another disagrees with them and for this reason kills the other becomes also an act that must within the frame and logic of giving precedence to one's human rights be tolerated. In all of this, where we see there is that which is right such as tolerance, and nothing that is wrong except that which is considered intolerance we return to another duality of nature and come to the concept that there is right and there is wrong. We construct for ourselves in a modern form a human jungle, where then it is the fittest by whatever means, survive, and where in such argumentation we find sophistry and intellectual dishonesty. This system of thought then destructs the quality of life for all of who exists in what one considers to be a civilized society, a place where we live free from fear of our fellow human beings and where we work together for the common good for all.

In the acceptance of tolerance as being right and the determining factor of that of one being of a civilized humanity one experiences here a conceptual dilemma. In tolerating the behaviour of one who steals or another who assuages their sexual desires with the very young person, a child and where too one considers that one's sexual desires is a mentally predetermined one, this makes it so that perhaps outside of the concept of tolerance as being right and intolerance as being wrong, nothing else can be so identified. It makes it so too, that the tolerant person cannot be intolerant of any other person, perhaps one who disagrees with them. In this therefore we see that tolerance has its boundaries and exists within some system of thought, and what then becomes a moral frame.

Three moral frames are provided here for the construct of a civilized society. The first from an unknown source and taught in schools in the middle decades of the twentieth century as a memory gem is "I shall pass this way but once, any good deed that I can do let me do it now for I shall not pass this way again". We see here good deeds and bad deeds, right and wrong, as we appreciate our mortality. The second which is the Kantian Imperative requires of an individual when they propose to perform any deed, to ask if that which they propose to do, can each person in the world do the same and it becomes a better one for all. We can consider here what happens when we all strive to be the fittest rather than being fit. The third which flows from the spirituality of seeking to be responsible useful and gracious, and where one seeks to be fit, rather than being the fittest is, "there is no perfection in this world, and that which we seek to do, but if one should err, it is better to do so in the pursuit of seeking to do right rather than in seeking to do wrong".

Within these frames of thought and the morality arising there from, the consequential actions taken in the determining of the superstructure of law and order that is created in the governance of the state and nation and the parameters wherein which people live their lives and which too we use to guide our own lives as individuals, we place ourselves on the path towards a wholly civilized society and world.

4.2. Issues of sexual morality

The continuity of human life and society exists within the frame of sexuality and occurs through heterosexual relationships, and which is the expression of all the Gods that are worshipped in this world of diversity and the diversity of nature that is found herein. This manner of procreation is so in the life of animals, the grouping of life within which we human beings are identified. A sexual morality is fundamental to our humanity, and to the continuing of our society as a civilized place not only in its physical dimension but also its mental and spiritual dimension. Heterosexuality is the dominant and norm of sexuality in which such desires are assuaged and one in which for the most part two adult persons of the opposite sex becomes attracted to each other and forms a relationship that not only satisfies their sexual desires but through this relationship the continuity of human beings in society. In western societies and within the frame of individualism the union of a male and a female person, is a matter of their own choice and is based on their attraction to each other, both spiritually, physically and materially. There are societies where the individual's choice of a partner in this union, considered a marriage, is not paramount. Marriage then is identified as a relationship of commitment between two persons of the opposite sex in which human beings in society is procreated as too the sexual desires of the partners in this relationship is assuaged.

In society we laud certain behaviour such as honesty; speaking the truth, and what we call decency, this being understood as doing to and for others that which we would wish them to do to, and for us. In honesty one can have trust in the behaviour of the person; in speaking the truth; that which one says can be relied upon and in decency we can be relied upon as one who does not seek to diminish another. These are behaviours which are in keeping with the Kantian Imperative, that if practiced by all human beings in this diverse universe it would facilitate the enhancement of well being and enabling an abiding peace and harmony in societies and with societies, even where we experience and worship God in different ways. These are actions with outcomes that enhance our human condition and situation both spiritually and materially lending then to the spiraling upwards of the quality of life of all. These actions therefore can be said to be right, and actions that deviates from these can be said to be wrong.

As an individual, one is able to recognize aberrant occurrences in nature, some of which are benign and some that are deleterious.

In human sexuality there occurs the attraction of two persons of the same sex, sufficiently so that they seek within a relationship for this purpose to assuage their sexuality. This relationship called a homosexual one, and is not general, but one that is more concerned with the assuaging of the aberrant and not normal sexual desires of the individuals in the relationship, whilst at the same time does not provide the procreation of human beings. It is within the situation of human sexuality today that we find the major moral issues, both within that of the norm of nature of heterosexuality and the not norm of homosexuality. In some Greek city states; before Christ; in seeking to make its people strong and to enable them to sustain themselves against all others, young people were educated in homosexuality and stealing. These city states did not last for a long time as they were destroyed by the citizens from within and by others from outside. In their demise we can recognize an affirmation of the Kantian Imperative which determines what is good and right and what is bad and wrong.

At a later date in our human history and at the writing of the Christian Bible we find the allegorical story of the demise of Sodom and Gomorrah as a consequence of the preponderance of homosexual behaviour there. One can appreciate that high levels of homosexuality provides a low level of the procreation of human beings and the capacity of the state nation to sustain and provide the people there the services that are required for its continuity and where and when any major natural disaster occurs, this then worsens the situation. In this too we can appreciate the interdependence of people within a state and society. The occurrence of homosexuality in society is considered now, more a matter of predetermination rather than predisposition, nor that of socialization as was in the earlier Greek societies. Implicit in this consideration is that there are women genetically and physically born to be attracted to other women, some in a feminine manner and others in a masculine manner, and to the extent that they seek such persons out in order to assuage their sexuality. An issue arises here for society in its law and order as to how this search is pursued for other persons of this not normal sexuality and how the assuaging of this is conducted. This situation is also found amongst men, some attracted to another man in a masculine manner and others attracted to others in a feminine manner. We find in society persons that are genetically and mentally challenged and they are not considered for studies to become rocket scientists. The question arises here of the level of this predetermination. Another dimension of this argument of predetermination is that one's gender classification, as that of being of a male physical structure or a female physical structure, is not that which identifies one's sexuality, but more that of a mental matter, this even as we accept that our human physical attributes determines our rights and capacity for survival. In all of this we come to the question as to what is considered pre- determination and what is predisposition, the levels of either, and what gives rise to how one expresses one's sexuality. Within the concept of predetermination and in the situation of homosexuality, it is known that this takes one to the end of a lineage and within the context of natural selection and the survival of the fittest this sexuality becomes the tool of nature for de-selection. Within the spirituality and system of thought of the survival of the fittest where one finds within a society the preponderance of homosexuality which can be construed as the de-selection of many people there and which then could lead to its destruct, that existing there, is some vector of humanity and behaviour that drives this, and such must necessarily be considered wrong, and immoral.

In the discussion today about the development of society it is considered that children are best raised in the family of their parents, a male the father and a female the mother, and the ideal family is one where these two persons are committed to each other through marriage. We now have it being considered that the human rights of individuals who are homosexuals who wish to have the assuaging of their sexuality within a committed partnership is being denied them when these person seek to do this in a legal frame, and which is to be considered a marriage. Accordingly we now have the concept of marriage, and importantly a situation where there are persons of the opposite sex and which for most part are able to provide for the continuity of human beings to be nurtured in the norms of society not any longer defining that, but more a relationship for the assuaging of one's not normal in nature sexuality and which makes for problems in communication and the first step towards a new society. This new society will be one where we have two persons of the same sex being a family, and later where this is not so already, rights will be granted to procure as they see fit a child to raise in this family, which will be of two females, two mothers, or that of two men, two fathers. Within this we find new directions for this new society.

Heterosexual relations provides not only for the assuaging of one's sexuality, but also the procreation and continuity of human beings and society. It is known that in the days of slavery in the Caribbean in the near past that to maintain the slave population and more so after trafficking of them as human capital and commodity from Africa had ceased, that there were selected heterosexual persons to provide the continuity of persons that could provide the labour service that was required on the plantations. It was a situation in which the life that flowed from the body of a woman, and which a male had been part of, was ultimately not the responsibility of these persons. It can be appreciated here that in the case of the female this was more distressing than that of the male as the child resided in the body of the female. In our society of today the release of distress such as that was, is sought in abortion. In many societies this approach to a woman releasing of distress in the procreating of human beings in society is considered in a negative manner and she is denied the ultimate responsibility for that which is nurtured within and flows from her body, and as in like manner that this occurred in the near past time of slavery in the Caribbean.

Within the situation of heterosexuality and that of homosexuality we find dilemmas for the governance of the state. In the pursuit of heterosexuality, we find in this, the procreation of human beings, aberrant occurrences that diminish this outcome whilst in the pursuit of homosexuality we recognize there, that it wholly does not contribute the procreation of human being. In the proclamation and acclamation of this sexuality as that which is the major dimension of one's humanity and the acceptance of this by others makes a contribution to society and its continuity, not only diminishes and demeans society, but these persons too. It diminishes and demeans these persons as in this proclamation and acclamation it places this dimension of their humanity which does not contribute either spiritually or materially to the society above that of others of their self and their humanity, so then they must be considered much less than others. Participatory democratic governance allows for the resolving of such a matter within the Kantian Imperative and where as is of nature and the transcendental, inexplicable and imponderable spirit, aberrant and dysfunctional situations arise.

Within a morality derived from the system of thought of the survival of the fit rather than that of the fittest, and where in the situation of homosexuals one would seek to identify the talents and competencies which they could use in the service to the nation this would place one on the path to being fit to survive. In like manner that the predetermined mentally challenged would not be directed to becoming a rocket scientist, so too would a homosexual, predetermined mentally or physically, would not be given the task to train the very young people about family life and the living together of a male and female within the norm of nature and from which we have the continuity of society. Other factors and dimension of their humanity would ultimately be considered in the determining of how they serve society and be served, and this firstly by themselves, and as a civilized person. It then will not be their sexuality that ultimately defines them, and the proclamation and acclamation of this, but the manner in which they use such talents as they have in the service of society and thereby being fit to survive.

In the governance of the state and nation and within a moral frame and system of thought of the survival of the fit, such issues are resolved in a manner that allows for the creating of a civilized society, and one of greater longevity.

4.3. Issues of business morality

Graciousness in business is more seen in its absence than in its presence. One will exploit opportunities rather than the satisfying of them through the optimizing of their occurrences and where the parties in this situation of service, the persons in this transaction and relationship of giving and receiving, finds an interconnection with each other and both becoming enriched. It is in business that we are interconnected as we seek our daily lives in society, and more so the one in which the struggle for survival of the fittest is predominant. The consequence of this is seen quite starkly between the nations that are considered rich and those considered poor, and where trade and business over time and the cumulative effect of this is that the material quality of life of the rich grows, whilst that of the poor has diminished over time. The relationship has not been pursued within a collaborative frame of the enhancing and enrichment of each other so as to sustain with continuity this relationship of service to each other, but within the frame of seeking the maximization of the situation which then leads to the diminishing of one or the other, and then moving on to another.

In collaborative relationships trust, learning and the appreciation of each other arises and which engenders even further relationships of enhancement, wherein the development of practices for each and their environment can be pursued, thereby providing to each a better quality of life, materially and spiritually. In this frame all the people in all societies are enriched as so too the world rather than the frame of maximizing benefits for one where fear is engendered and where in this situation and struggle not to be diminished our creative energies are used to manipulate all factors therein. In pursuit of this we come to recognize that this is best done when we depersonalize even the human dimensions there and which has brought us to think of the persons that are served as markets and the persons that do so as human assets and capital.

At the individual level where we serve each other we do not generally recognize this as being useful. We see this as conducting business which for most is considered an amoral endeavour, as is to be construed as business is business and also should never be conducted at a place of worship, which is a holy place. It is not considered that the ultimate expression of God in man is how we serve each other in our daily lives and that is done through the vehicle of business wherein which, as we serve we obtain our rewards that enables our material sustenance and our survival. The pursuit of business, that of using our talents and skills in serving our fellow human beings is generally not done within the frame of friendship because of the over riding fear of failure in the transaction and consequential breach of trust. In the pursuit of business within the system of thought of the survival of the fittest and where there is the embedded behaviour of the diminishing of one for the benefit of the other and when we do this to persons whom we consider friends we appreciate in this how we spiritually diminish our humanity, and human relationships, and life in society. We are collectively poorer for this, as we find here individualism and self interest above and beyond service for equitable reward, and the absence of graciousness.

It is in business where we use our talents and creativity to serve others and be rewarded that the most fertile ground for graciousness exists, and from which we create a civilized society. No individual stands alone, though one may well stand detached, nor does a community within a nation, or a nation within the world, and our humanity and self is determined by this reality. When we do business with each other, an interaction that focuses on our material sustenance and which ultimately contributes to our survival, and when we do this in a manner that enriches both ourselves and the others with whom we interact, we create the ground not only for our survival, but for the enhancement of our humanity. This will cause fear to be diminished and trust and graciousness engendered, thereby providing to both a highly satisfactory quality of life, both materially and spiritually and also the prolonging and the continuity of such.

We are being useful when we play a part in serving each other not only in providing to each other corn and wheat, rice and potatoes and peppers, and pots and pans but also in the service of teaching, in the healing of the sick, not only by the drugs we make but also in the diagnosing of the illness by doctors and the nursing by nurses; and as also one serves within the structure and systems of state governance where the laws of the state are created such as those that guide us as to how we build our houses, the physical structure within which we live our lives. All these activities are production endeavours and part of which provides us with the quality of life we enjoy and which determines our humanity. Business arises out of all these activities of human intercourse, some of these being the business of the state, others through that of the enterprise of individuals, and to the extent that we in these relationships not only serve each other and society but seek to enrich each situation, we engender graciousness in our selves and humanity.

When we pursue business in the context of a morality coming from a system of thought of the survival of the fittest and our consequential rights, we place ourselves on a path that leads us to the diminishing of others and society and ultimately ourselves. When we conduct business in the context of a morality coming from a system of thought of the survival of the fit and consequential responsibility, we place ourselves on the path to the enhancement and enrichment of society where we have choice and diversity. In this we acknowledge God's grace in the creating of this diversity. When we ourselves in accepting His transcendental authority and wisdom do likewise in the displaying of graciousness to this diversity, we enhance our own selves, our humanity and then the world.

4.4. Issues of religion and morality

In the western world and in the early years of the twentieth century and to its midpoint, it was so that in the education of its citizens; the youngest of children; in the first schools of their attendance which were for the most part state schools, children then were exposed to religious worship and the instruction in the Christian religion as was dominant there. There were children there from diverse mainstream religions as too from the diverse form of worshipping within the Christian religion and in time problems and conflicts arose there in conduct of the worshipping of God; the Transcendental, Imponderable and Inexplicable spirit. In the foiling of the ascendancy of one form of worship over the other, and too one religion over the other, and as is within the embedded spirituality and behaviour of people who live within the mantra of the survival of the fittest not to be the loser, the teaching of a religious faith and the moral behaviour that existed within religion was removed from schools.

A victory for irreligiousness occurred and consequential amorality at best and immorality at worst, and a situation in which all became losers rather than winners. Society lost as a consequence of the absence of a situation in which there was no clear and certain point in the life of young person where their humanity was impacted upon within any moral frame. Commencing then, this has impacted on the young people then and who now are adults. For this reason then we find in the main persons without a defined morality or value system, but mostly an unconscious and unwitting one, this being that which is derived from the mantra of the survival of the fittest, and out of which we experience much of the behaviour of people in society today. In most societies now there exists no organization outside of religious one which provides any moral frame for its diverse people to live within except that which is embedded and provided by the law and order there. Within this spiritual vacuum when we find a law and order that emphasizes the physical dimension of our selves by providing to each what is considered rights as a consequence of them being of the human specie and without any concern for their conduct, this then emphasizing their physical and material self without any concern for their mental self from which flows our humanity, we come unwittingly to the situation which we find now in society. This default spirituality and morality that takes the place of that which was provided by religion at earlier times, that of the survival of the fittest is to be seen as reflected even in societies of high material well being where there is to be found, a pervasive lack of trust and fear of one's fellow human beings, as too the increasing levels of crime and violence, this characteristic being that which for the most part identifies the poorer nations.

There are many religions in this world and within each there are differences. From Judaism we have Christianity, and within the Christians we have the Catholics and Protestants. Within the Protestants we have the Episcopalians and the Baptists and within these there are further divisions. All of these recognize and worship God differently, and this within what we consider to be a mainstream religion, that of Christianity. There exist other mainstream religions such as Islam, Buddhism and Hinduism, to name a few. A commonality of religion is that they are derived from the recognition that human beings are a small part of this diverse universe and of our not-knowingness of much that drives it. Recognition comes too that the total force that drives it transcend our inputs, even as we are aware that it has it impacts, parallel to God's force which we identify as nature. This transcendental and spiritual force is identified as God towards whom one humbles one's self in worship. This Spiritual God is attributed capabilities that human beings given their environment wishes Him to have so as to enable them to be in a relationship with this one who is the ultimate enabling force for their survival. Another vector of commonality is that of human beings coming to terms with this transcendental force and recognizing patterns of outcomes from certain actions that are for the most part reliable and predictable and which affords them their existence, which then develops in them trust and faith in this spirit.

Within this mental and spiritual dimension of our humanity there are recognized actions that provide the consequences that are sought for our life and living and therefore considered right, and actions that do not do so and are considered wrong. This then becomes our relationship with God out of which is developed a term of reference for living and a morality. The providing to individuals within their education in their early life, the understanding that religion is about the commonality of our humanity of not-knowingness of the transcendental, inexplicable and imponderable force within this universe of ours in which we exist and experience in diverse ways, engenders graciousness within their humanity. One then goes further, and provide to the young children, the adults of tomorrow, with a morality that transcends religion and where there is to be found for all people, that which is right and that which is wrong, and in this enhance their life not only as individuals in societies and nation state, and thereby construct a civilized nation state, but within what then becomes a civilized and diverse universe.

4.5. Issue of responsibility through social apprenticeship.

Schools provided in the nineteenth and the greater part of the twentieth century, individuals in the western societies generally with education and training. Education not only honed the skills of reasoning but also provided a value system and morality which gave one a term of reference in which to live one's life. In education therefore, one had instruction in religion, and in Caribbean schools one learned what was called "memory gems", such as "to be polite is to do or say this kindest things in the kindest ways", and another and as earlier stated, "I shall pass this way but once, any good deed that I can do let me do it now for I shall not pass this way again", such therefore providing a basis for interpersonal relationships with our fellow human beings in society. These rules of behaviour enables us to recognize that even within the system of thought of the survival of the fittest, all life was not about might being right, and that there existed other vectors of thought for relating with each other and which enabled kindliness and graciousness in our lives, and which enriched it.

Schools moved away from education to more that of training and even in tertiary level educational institutions where one obtained the highest level of education, the mix of this was more that of training than of education in which our faculty for reason is engaged and honed. Training is that which enables one to become human assets and capital quickly through obtaining immediately the skills and competencies required for undertaking the tasks we must perform in society and from which we obtain our material sustenance. This training and skill development is provided for the most part without any broad frame of reference, sometimes not even in respect of how one skill is proximate to another or situate in its genre and in society, but within the narrow frame of it being marketable, and it having the capacity to attract to it the highest of material rewards from society. It is in this mode which determines our humanity that we find our place in society, void of much capacity and desire for reasoning and any spirituality and terms of morality that arises in the greatest measure from education. In the endeavours of training that allows us to obtain as quickly as possible the material well being we seek, we consequently then measure our self worth and the success of our now depersonalized, commoditized and commercialized selves, where service and usefulness in society is not a concern, nor a spiritual well being of such, but by a material well being that is expressed at the individual level, by the of personal possessions of things that are sometimes grandiose and attention attracting.

Institutions of education when they move away from the providing to individuals the ground for the development of the terms of reference and or a system of thought that provides a basis for our living together, becomes places of amorality and leaves the society without any certain place for the spiritual development of individual as civilized citizens. Within the frame of rights however each individual as a child is provided free education which is for the most part an amoral one and one too that is more that of training. In this we return to what was the norm in older societies, even some of those we consider primitive, where what was considered important then for individuals in society to know, was provided to all young people free of cost to them. In returning to the lasting wisdom of the past of providing education to all and free, this would be done within the frame of the knowledge and experiences we have gained in the evolving of societies and where we have come to appreciate that what we have as our humanity; language, fears hopes, joys, religion; is a function of that which has been bequeathed to them by their forbears through the transcendental, imponderable and inexplicable spirit of God and of nature. In this we find the morality of responsibility and usefulness where, in having received it becomes then their duty to give and to serve as they have been served. During the time that they are then being served further by being provided with an education, the underlying system of thought and morality of society would be a dimension of this. With the evolving and recognition that our society is placed on the path of construct to that of a civilized one within the system of thought and morality of the survival of the fit, this then would be the underlying thoughts in the process and structure of education.

In the process of the educating of children of society and of a morality of serving and being served this could be within what could be considered a system of social apprenticeship. Today's society is more complex than that of yesterday, the past, where there was then generally and in most societies one level of education which then was seen more as the rites of passage, and we now have three levels. These are identified as the primary level, the secondary level and the tertiary level. The reality is that in societies of today a child is not kept at home with a parent but goes to what is considered a basic school and so what one has in society is four levels of education. The secondary level is the one that takes the child to the point where one is ready to go into the world of work and to earn one's living. It is at this secondary level of education and later the tertiary level, in the lives of these young citizens that the fundamental spiritual value of that of contributing and being of service to society from which one obtained one's humanity is best engendered, and out of which would come the acceptance of a morality of responsibility, and the consequential behaviour of service to one's fellow human beings in society. At the pre – secondary levels of education and the teaching of the basic subjects of reading, writing and calculating when this is done in a manner that enable these young person to appreciate during the learning of concepts, and ideas there of what it is to be responsible and useful in being able to contribute and as they receive, it deepens the possibility for the enhancement of the lives of these persons in society. Over time, and as the concept and humanity of responsibility, usefulness and graciousness through service to others becomes the dominant dimension of the morality and behaviour of individuals replacing that of the survival of the fittest, individualism and rights, to that of the survival of the fit, this system of thought which engenders collaborative and creative actions, it will be so that society moves towards becoming a highly civilized one, where there will be a high level of freedom of fear from one's fellow citizens.

A commencing step to this end would be that of social apprenticeship, particularly in the instances where education is made free, beginning from the secondary level of education at the final years of their studies there. This would be that students are assigned tasks that require very low level skills and competencies in society, such as the keeping of the streets clean, perhaps the maintaining of the offices in which persons who serve in the governance of the state or the offices of other state organization where the work of the state is pursued, in hospitals, in restaurants, all these being tasks that enhances the ambience in which people serve and consequentially, the people there. In this these young persons serve as they serve. In the certification of graduation from secondary level educational institutions, how well these students serve there, their behaviour to others and too the manner in which they perform their task will be part of this. One envisages here the creating of a level of flexibility in serving in these jobs and too a flexibility in teaching. It may well be that in this process of the educating of the young people in society of the morality of serve and be served and finding usefulness and self worth in these jobs, that there be found those who will take this path out of aberrant and dysfunctional situations where they do not obtain within the circumstances and sphere in which they then live all the material well being they require such as food and clothes, and they extend their service in this apprenticeship role to correct such dysfunctions then in their lives. This could also be a path for others who wish to go to the further and higher level of tertiary education.

Within this system of thought of the survival of the fit, and from which the humanity of responsibility, usefulness and graciousness arise that one's life has meaning, social apprenticeship becomes a tool to deepen in this humanity of the people there and where society then travels on the path with continuity of being civilized. In society where the least of jobs there provides individuals there with first of all self worth, being fit to survive, and both a material and a spiritual well being, it creates in them too, a sense of humility as it then goes further and enhances the quality of life there for all.

Over time and as society evolves in a spiraling upwards manner the social apprenticeship tasks will change and as too we all become more educated and appreciate each other more and the role each plays in society, we will relate to each other not within the frame of rights and forbearance flowing from the system of thought of the survival of the fittest, but more so within that of the fit. It is in that frame that we find the morality of responsibility, usefulness and graciousness which leads to the construct of a society of highly civilized people where service to each other is the dominant dimension of their self rather than of receiving within the frame of rights.

4.6. Contemporary Caribbean civilization and morality

We have had many civilizations out of which have arisen different societies. The original Caribbean community and civilization have been completely destroyed by western civilization and societies in the pursuit of life and living within the system of thought of the survival of the fittest. This act within that system of thought has brought us from diverse parts of the world to this Caribbean land that is considered to be one of the more wonderful parts of the creation of this universe, and that of God, that spirit and force that is above and beyond us all. In the sharing of our existence in the space of these small islands to which we have brought our diversity of humanity as is expressed in our diverse images of God and consequential religion, the ground has been provided for us to appreciate each other through the communal and collective participation in endeavours that have enabled our survival as a talented and creative people.

We the Caribbean people stand now on the threshold of being a new and civilized community which is situate at the cross roads of the journey between the north and the south, and the east and the west in this world. As we now ponder the pursuit of our lives and build our new society we give thought of doing so, not within the system of thought of the survival of the fittest as was the underlying moral value then and which enabled the destroying our predecessors on this land, but seek now to do so within the system of though and morality of the survival of the fit. We accept each other as being fit as our God, all our Gods have placed us here together by Their will, and this adjustment and accommodation to each other becomes the expression of this transcendental, imponderable and inexplicable spirit within which we are able to survive. This spirit within which we all will live our lives comes nearer to the experience we have of nature that we find around us, as we first see in our diverse selves, and in the realities of the diverse environment, beginning in our near physical space and extending to the other parts of the universe from which we have come to be here. Out of this acceptance of the survival of the fit, in the experiencing of our diverse humanity and our ultimate not-knowingness, we come to the morality of responsibility, usefulness and graciousness to each other as the system of thought within which we pursue our endeavours and relationship in the creating with continuity our new Caribbean civilization.

We begin first within the governance of our nation state to create structures that engenders the system of thought and moral values of responsibility usefulness and graciousness where we engage ourselves collectively and in a collaborative style. This will be one where we come as close as possible to the hearing of all of the voices of the people of society and which then is part of the creating of the law and order in which we live our lives and then the policies of our state organizations, all of this then determining our consequential humanity. It will be one where we use iron not to make guns in order for us to free ourselves from fear of our fellow human beings, but to make ploughs to plant corn to feed ourselves, and cotton to make clothes, and as we enjoy our lives as we serve each other.

Upon the Caribbean ground of existence it is concluded that from God we receive life, and then from our fellow human beings, our humanity, which gives us a debt of gratitude and consequential responsibility first to them. When we work together and equitably share with our near and far community that which we have produced, we enrich ourselves and the world. It is in this discharge that we as individuals obtain rights; considered as civil and in which our physical and material self is connected to our mental and spiritual self; and are fit to survive.

Within the morality and pursuit of responsibility which engenders in us usefulness and graciousness we create first a civilized community and then, world, rather than in the enforcement of forbearance in the pursuit of what is considered our human rights and which is concerned only with our physical and material self. When we deliberately discharge this responsibility in a collective and collaborative manner, we deepen our humanity in this moral frame as we enhance further our human situation and give greater meaning and purpose to our lives

EPILOGUE

We as individuals have no ultimate and final answers as to how the universe came to be, and ourselves too, as part of this. We have developed a concept of that of perfection in matters spiritual and physical that we have never achieved. We have accepted in the pursuit of perfection our lives over time have improved and become less troubling. We know this too, that when we improve our situation we have a feeling that is satisfying and energize us. We know also that when many of us have that feeling in the presence of each other we find life worth the while living.

When we therefore place more into the enhancing of life and living we find meaning in our life, and that it is better for us all. When we take out without putting in, some may well feel then that all is well with them, but for most they lose self worth and satisfaction. It is this spirit that causes us to seek to prove our worth as that of above and beyond others, even by showing our capacity to destroy that which we find around us. The reality is that we can never destroy all and most likely will destroy one's self in seeking to do so. We know too that in the history of our human existence that it is in acting to build rather than to destroy that we create the places where we exist, and that within these places we must give guidance in this to others, through knowing what enhances and what does not. In this we have what is right and what is wrong, and from which flows our rights.

Demeaning, diminishing and the destroying of things give no positive meaning in life and living. It is a spirituality of responsibility that allows for collaborative endeavours with others in being creative, and this within the moral frame of usefulness and graciousness that does so. This gives too with continuity, peace and a positive power in one's self and soul, and allows for purpose and meaning in one's life. This has been my experience.

ABOUT THE AUTHOR

The author was born in Jamaica and had his early education there at the Half Way Tree Elementary School where he was influenced by educators there at the school such as the Headmaster Mr. Wesley James and his wife Mrs. Edith Dalton-James. Later at the Kingston Technical High School he came under the influence of Messrs H. Atkins, J. Wray and S. Vaughan, who one day on asking why I was late for classes upon hearing my excuse for this advised that the persons who makes good excuses, makes nothing else that is good.

He migrated to the UK in the late nineteen fifties and completed studies in Business at the Balham & Tooting College of Commerce, now the South West London College of Commerce. After this he did post graduate studies in Human Resource Management in the Department of Business at Strathclyde University, now the Strathclyde University School of Business.

He then went to Zambia where he lectured at the Evelyn Hone College of Further Education and later at the Mindolo Ecumenical Foundation where he established there executive development courses. It was there that he met a Swedish born lady who became his fiance'e. On leaving Zambia he returned to UK to do further post graduate studies in Management at Brighton Polytechnic, which later became Brighton University.

He returned to Jamaica after this, married his fiance'e and worked in the field of Human Resource Management. Later he lectured at the University of Technology and became Senior

Lecturer in charge of the Management Division in the Faculty of Business Administration from which he retired. At UTech he was part of a team that designed, developed and implemented the Bachelors degree in Human Resource Management and helped in the laying of the ground for the Bachelors degree in Operations Management.

He now spends his time between Jamaica and Sweden with his wife, three adult children and now five grandchildren there.

www.ingramcontent.com/pod-product-compliance
Lightning Source LLC
Chambersburg PA
CBHW060827050426
42453CB00008B/611